FIFTY FIRST DATES

This edition published by
Moore Digital Media
P.O. Box 480400
Los Angeles, CA 90048

(This was previously published under the title Crazy. Beautiful. Love. parts
i & ii).

This memoir is a work of nonfiction. Nonetheless all names, some identifying
details, and personal characteristics have been changed.

The author acknowledges the trademarked status and trademark owners of
various products referenced in this work of fiction, which have been used
without permission. The publication/use of these trademarks is not
authorized, associated with, or sponsored by the trademark owners.
Cover: Jocelyn Grant

ISBN: 978-1-64414-003-1

Also by Jolie Moore

Maybe Baby

Maybe Him

Maybe Again

Maybe Now

Maybe You

Taming the Bad Boy

Someone Else's Wife

The Secrets She Keeps

Her Secret Crush

What Was Perfect

What Was Lost

What Was True

Release

Fifty First Dates (*a memoir*)

FIFTY FIRST DATES

A Crazy Beautiful Love Story

JOLIE MOORE

Falling in love is much more exciting to me than swiping right.

—The Foreigner

Preface

Dan Savage ruined my marriage, but saved my life.

I go through a lot of phases where I zero in on a certain area of interest. For a few months, it will be all biographies—reading the Clarence Thomas and Anita Hill memoirs back to back was an amazing brain exercise.

Another month it will be a binge on research into the Los Angeles public schools—even though I don't have a child in school there.

The impact of World War II on northern Africa was an esoteric, but fascinating one as well.

For the last few years, on and off, I've been obsessed with advice columns. Which led to a similar interest in advice podcasts. This dovetailed with my podcast obsession nicely and kept drives and dog walks from bouncing between wall to wall comedians and women's fiction audiobooks.

Maybe four or five years ago, I can't remember exactly when, I started listening to back episodes of the Savage Lovecast. For those three people who don't know, it's a podcast where Dan Savage—an out gay man—gives sex and relationship advice to straight and gay alike.

Although I'm an author of romance and women's fiction (both with lots of sex), what I knew about sex and relationships before tuning into the podcast and reading Savage's columns in *The Stranger* could have fit in a thimble.

A very tiny thimble, far too small for my fingers.

A decorative thimble, really.

The kind of thimble that my grandmother's friends used to collect and showcase in their curio cabinets. Did I mention I once knew a guy who specialized in the importation of curio cabinets? Totally fascinating line of work. But as always, I digress from the hard stuff I'm trying to say.

I'm one hundred percent sure that if you asked my mother, she would say that she was very open about sex and relationships. I'm sure because that's what she'd tell you. Right after telling you she was a Ph.D. and the world's greatest mother. The former is true, the latter, not so much because in my experience alcoholic narcissists are not great at nurturing.

But I stepped out into the world—or college that is— thinking I knew all there was to know about sex and relationships. Even though I'd never seen a successful heterosexual, or even homosexual relationship up close and personal. I'd had my mother who gave me a talk on the birds and bees at five and Harlequin romance, which comprised the entire rest of my education.

That, it turns out, was woefully inadequate. In case you're wondering, I got my birds-and-bees talk one night when my mother was straightening my hair with a hot comb (back when that was a thing). My five-year-old self innocently asked her where babies came from. Because I'm an only child of only children I'd never see my mother or any family members pregnant. I can't say why, but the question crossed my child mind that day.

The explanation I got was fairly clinical about—well you know—penises and vaginas and fertilization. I remember being so shocked that I ran upstairs and asked my grandmother. She confirmed it and I had to spend some time integrating that knowledge.

Years later, I did ask my mother why she'd gave me so much information at age five. The answer was that my grandfather was a pedophile who had abused her. Any explanation as to why we lived with him and why I'd been left alone with him lots and lots of times was never forthcoming.

What I'm getting at is that no one ever talked to me about sex outside of rudimentary mechanics. That it felt good. That women deserved to get pleasure from it. That it didn't have to—and in fact—shouldn't hurt. My mother never told me that. Neither of my grandmothers did. But Dan Savage was happy to lay it out there. I hate to say it, but my past thirty-five-year-old self, my self who had been married, at that point, for more than a dozen years was flabbergasted.

In the back of my mind, I guess I knew about women's agency. I mean, I wrote about it every single day. But I'd never experienced it myself. I had no idea that sexual compatibility could or should be one of the most important elements of a relationship until he'd mentioned it for the first or five thousandth time in his column and podcast.

What my brain asked?

My mind exploded with that single question.

I didn't have to have sex because my husband worked outside the home and paid the bills. I didn't have to have sex that hurt or didn't excite me or felt degrading. It was a fucking revelation. That little kernel was like an irritation to the oyster. I added some therapy on top, and a pearl was born.

I walked out on a marriage of many years with an emotionally and sometimes physically abusive husband because I could. Because I deserved more both in and out of the bedroom. Now all I have to do is figure out how to get it.

Introduction

It took everything I had to walk out on him. For years, I'd lived in dread. Dread of him coming home from work angry. Dread of him screaming at me. Dread of him threatening to kill us all while driving like a maniac on the freeway.

One day, though, I'd had enough. I opened my own bank account and tucked away money one month at a time. I searched for an apartment in West Hollywood during the day while he was at work. I packed myself an overnight bag and kept it in the back of my SUV...my getaway car. Hired a moving van and did it. It was both the hardest and the easiest thing I'd ever done.

For months, I sat in my apartment and cried. I cried over the mistakes I'd made for staying in a relationship too long. I cried for the years I'd lost.

One day, I was done crying. I may not have found my forever guy this last time or any of the times before that. But I know there's a guy out there for me. So I signed up for Bumble, and OkCupid, and even Tinder.

What follows are stories of the fifty first dates that I hope will lead me to finding my new love.

My own Crazy. Beautiful. Love. Story.

ONE

The Drummer Boy

JANUARY 12.

WHEN I GOT to the bar it was 8:15 PM. Big plastic tarps covered everything outside. The warm and cozy fire pits, looking into my date's eyes over the glow of orange flame? Neither of those was going to happen.

Those plans had fizzled with the latest winter storm. It hardly ever rains in Southern California, but my first date came on a night when it had been raining for three solid days. It was too late to pick somewhere new so I went inside the cozy little restaurant interior I'd never seen.

I was the only patron.

"No one comes out when it rains," the waiter said to me as he told me I could sit at any of the ten or so vacant tables.

I picked a table in a dark corner and ordered a glass of pinot noir. I hoped that it would take the edge off my nerves because this being my first date in years had given me a big 'ol case of nerves.

When it rains in Los Angeles the traffic snarls. I took out my Kindle and read after I got a text from Drummer Boy saying he was running late. By 8:45, he was there. He looked exactly like his picture. Medium height, broad shoulders, one hell of a chest, and lots of long black hair.

I should tell you now that I have a type. Every guy has to be at least three of these things. If he hits all five, well then Yahtzee.

1. Cute.
2. Long hair. My first high school crush had long hair. What can I say?
3. Musician or other creative pursuit. I love musicians, writers, visual artists, and film makers the best.
4. At least medium build. I don't like weighing more than a guy. I'm short so height doesn't matter as much.
5. A good kisser. Now this is one that requires experimentation. But I'm game.

Drummer Boy was batting four for five when he came to the table. I stood to welcome him, and instead of shaking my hand, or bussing me on the cheek, he immediately wrapped me in a bear hug.

"I'm a hugger," he said as he let me go oh-slow-slowly. He made no secret that he was checking me out. From his smile, I think I made the grade.

He smelled good. That was a definite bonus. I sat and closed my ereader and put it and my phone in my purse because it was looking like he was going to be all the entertainment I needed. The bartender got him his own glass of pinot.

"So you write romance?" he asked.

I nodded. I'd put my job on my online dating profile. I braced myself ready for the usual question I got from random people on the street, usually asked with a wink, a nod, and an elbow nudge about how I do my research. Drummer Boy didn't ask anything else. So I turned the tables.

"And you bang the drums?"

His main work was as a session musician. He talked about working on various movies and for some of the most popular recording artists today. Not that I'd heard of all of them. Some I had to Google much, much later.

Turns out many were famous, just not known to me. Writing at home all day in silence didn't expose me to as much pop culture as most people.

"Do you drink coffee or tea?" he asked when the waiter brought a dessert menu.

"I can't do caffeine at night. But in the mornings I drink tea. Actually I get my tea from an Indian spice shop," I said. "I like strong, loose leaf, spiced tea."

"Indian spice shop?" A single dark eyebrow rose in question.

"In Los Feliz. It's a perk of colonialism I guess."

Drummer Boy's laugh was big and hearty. "Yes that's something I know quite a lot about."

Drummer Boy knew a lot about colonialism because he was Native American. It's why his black hair was long. It was a cultural thing, not the usual musician's defiance of authority. I took long hair for any reason.

We talked more about music in general. I knew he was a keeper when he agreed that Alanis Morisette's *Jagged Little Pill* is still the best album ever. He told me a lot about his tribe and growing as a Native American in the South Bay area of Los Angeles county.

The wine was good. The chocolate and banana bread pudding dessert we shared was even better.

Before I knew it more than three hours had passed and the bartenders were making a last call. They wanted to pack it in early because only one other couple had come in all night. I'm sure our wine and their appetizers had hardly covered the cost of the five wait staff hovering over their phones behind the bar.

"Can I walk you to your car?" Drummer Boy asked after he'd paid the bill. I offered to chip in or pay, but he waved me off saying this night was going to be his treat.

When I stood up from the table this time, his hug was a lot more familiar and included a brush of lips across my cheek. That contact sent shivers up and down my spine.

Buzzed on a large glass of strong wine and at least two years of no sex, I took him up on his offer to walk me the half block to my car because I had no idea what would come next or how to get to what I think I wanted to come next.

What came next was the best first kiss I've had in a long time. The last line of my online dating profile had the following line, 'Swipe left if you don't like kissing.' My ex didn't like kissing and I'd missed that more than other types of affection that had been lacking in our relationship.

Drummer Boy obviously very much liked kissing. So we did —up against my cold wet SUV while well dressed twenty somethings getting ready to go clubbing stood in a long line at the garishly lit Wells Fargo ATM. Having had enough of being watched and whistled at by them, I finally pulled the magic words from the deep recesses of my brain and spoke them aloud.

"Why don't you come back to my place?"

Our foreheads together, rapidly breathing each other's air, I texted him directions to my building.

I got into my car and in a huge hurry and not the least bit mindful of California's traffic laws, made a huge illegal U-turn on six-lane Fairfax Avenue. In five minutes my car was tucked safely in my designated spot and I was in my apartment.

Parking in West Hollywood at night is a huge nightmare so I knew it would take some time before Drummer Boy showed up at my front door. While I waited I turned off some of the brighter lights and took the lighter to a few candles.

"Even your socks are cute," Drummer Boy said after he'd finally come through the door. He shucked his own jacket and boots and got comfortable on my couch.

I'd been wearing mid-calf black leather boots earlier. They were the only thing I'd taken off when I'd come home.

"You're amazingly sexy," he offered looking me up and down. My body tingled with the way his eyes roamed. No one had looked at me that way in a long time.

I smiled at a loss to what to say to that compliment. Instead I sat next to him on my couch and took a hit of the vape pen he offered. He didn't waste any time.

In a second his lips were covering mine again. His hands were everywhere, caressing my stomach under my cashmere sweater and my ass through my velvet pants.

After long minutes of his caresses doing all sorts of amazing things to my body, I stood, took his hand, and led him to my bedroom. I couldn't wait for what was going to come next. My instincts were telling me it was going to be good.

What came next was mostly satisfying. Drummer Boy had an oral fixation. I enjoy oral. I think I enjoy it a lot. But it's not the only thing I wanted. The one thing I'd missed in my marriage was penetration. Because my ex husband was my first, I'd never had what I'd read about, hell, written about. I'd never been pounded by a guy. I really wanted to experience that. My ex was one pump, maybe, two, then he was done. Never more than a few seconds, tops.

After my third or fourth orgasm, I rooted around in my bedside table and pulled out one of the three pack of condoms I'd bought at the drug store the week before.

"I'm not hard, yet," he said.

I zeroed in on his cock. It was only semi hard. I took the initiative and fisted it. I stroked until his breath was uneven and he was hard. I handed him a condom and he rolled it on. Another pump or two from him and he was ready. I lay back again and opened for him. He entered me and it felt good. Really good. It only lasted for a couple of minutes though.

"I can't stay hard," he said before he pulled out. "But I can make you feel good."

He lay next to me and took my breasts in his hands. He tweaked each nipple, hard. I loved nipple play, but his pinch was on that border between pain and pleasure. I fell mute, though. I knew I should have told him the way I wanted to be touched, needed to be massaged, but I felt inhibited. After years of being silent, I didn't know how to find my voice. So I let him go down on me for a few more orgasms.

It was both pleasurable and exhausting at the same time. I kind of wanted a second chance to get more of what I wanted, give him more of what he needed. That would violate the rules of the one night stand, though. I knew enough about how this played out to understand that.

"You smell and taste amazing," he said hours after he arrived and laid back against my pillows.

It hadn't been exactly what I'd imagined, but had been what I'd needed to break my celibate streak. I looked at the leather cord around his neck, the only thing that he'd left on after all his clothes had come off. Two feathers hung from it. One gold. One silver.

"What are the feathers for?"

"My father gave this to me," he started. He fingered them. They caught and shone in the bedside light. "One is for courage. The other protection."

"Well you don't need protection from me," I said and kissed him again. Hours later we lay sated and exhausted. For someone nearing forty he had the stamina of a man nearly ten years younger.

"Don't fall in love with me," he implored as the dark and quiet night of West Hollywood settled all round us.

I paused for a moment and looked at him all bronze skin and amazing cheekbones. I liked him well enough to kiss him, and invite him to my apartment, and even to have sex with him. But this was my first date after getting out of a long term relationship. I wanted more.

To meet more people.

Have more experiences.

Do more kissing.

"There's no worry of that," I promised.

TWO

The Ski Bum

YOU EVER HAVE a date so boring that you forget about it? After I wrote all about Drummer Boy I realized I'd had another date the day before that had completely slipped my mind. That was my real first date.

OkCupid had matched me with him when I first signed up for the app. He was a self-described ski bum. That sounded interesting or at least more interesting than the other profiles I'd come across during my first week of swiping mostly left and sometimes right on three different apps.

At this point, I hadn't had sex for at least two years that I could remember and maybe far longer than that. My ex's idea of sex had been for him to watch porn, his iPad propped on his belly, while I gave him a hand or blow job.

Or if not the iPad, then his vintage Playboy magazines, his favorite playmates marked with handwritten annotated post-it notes. And yes, I was to pause so he could flip from one page to another.

So by the time I'd sorted through all those profiles and had set up a date, I was dying for it. I figured if The Ski Bum were halfway decent, I'd invite him back to my place for sex on a

Friday afternoon. Didn't sex in the afternoon used to be a thing?

He was a guy who lived in a downtown loft and took off on Thursdays for the slopes. A quick fantasy of me in a firelit ski lodge fizzed through my brain. I may not ski (because going downhill really fast scares the bejesus out of me), or do roller-coasters or anything like that, but I could whip up a mad fire-side fantasy scenario in my imagination.

I may not ski, but I'm a great ride or die companion and would happily road trip to the mountains where I could read my feet next to a toasty hearth or write next to a frost laden window while waiting for him to come back from the slopes. After our date, though, it was clear that those fantasies were destined to remain just that...fantasies.

Turned out skiing was the most interesting thing about him.

Let me tell you about the good part, though, before I get too far down the rabbit hole of all that went wrong with that first date.

I'd heard that men lie about their height on these dating sites. Since I'm only five feet two inches, though, I don't care as much about height as other women. Also, past forty, I don't wear heels as much as I used to.

Ski Bum was the full six foot something he'd put on his profile. He was tall. Unfortunately, he only hit one of my criteria and that was long hair. He took a hell of a good picture, because he was cuter in it than in person.

I think he was South Asian, but held himself like a Parisian. In any moment, I expected him to pull out a Gauloises cigarette and puff away contentedly while looking down his aristocratic nose at us Americans swilling what we considered to be coffee.

I met him in a coffee shop in Larchmont, a cute street of

shopping, restaurants, juice bars, and yoga in Los Angeles. I was early. He was late.

(Theme here? Guys! Be on time for dates. It's the least bit of respect you can show!)

I got a peppermint tea. It's the perfect date drink at a coffee bar. The mint saves you from coffee breath and the lack of caffeine saves you from amping up the nerves.

I sat and sipped and people watched while I waited. He showed up in a suit with shorts. Yeah, you got that right, it was a khaki suit with shorts instead of pants. I had zero idea what to make of that. But I'd already driven the ten minutes to get there and spent ten minutes parking, not to mention the ten plus minutes holding down a table, so I was in—short pants and all.

Ski Bum had indeed been skiing that morning. When I asked about it, I didn't get many answers except that it had been mostly good and a fortunate traffic-free ride home.

Can we digress another moment?

There was this story I heard on *This American Life* about five and a half years ago. In it reporter Sarah Koenig (of later *Serial* fame) interviews her mother about seven topics that should be off limits in conversation. One topic was traffic. So the five minute digression in what it was like to drive to Los Angeles from places east was not confidence inspiring.

I crossed my fingers hoping the rest of the conversation took a turn for the interesting. That hope was in vain because he launched into the speech I'm starting to think of as the 'vote of no confidence' speech. It was, unfortunately, to become a recurring theme in later dates.

He liked his job alright but was bummed that he'd ended up in the county tax office as his full time job instead of at an exciting dot-com. His apartment wasn't perfect. He'd moved every year of the last ten looking for the ideal place, and he'd yet to find it.

Oh, and he needed to sell an armoire. It was such a hassle selling this amazing piece of two hundred pound piece craftsmanship because no one in our very shallow and superficial city appreciated *real* furniture.

Oh, and he was going to spend his weekend helping out his elderly father who lived near the beach. That last was the most interesting thing about him. That he loved his dad and was willing to spend his off time helping the older man.

He asked me a little about writing romance but didn't think much of it. I used to give the four billion dollar female-powered industry spiel. But not anymore. I am not going to apologize for supporting myself with a job I love that keeps thousands of readers happy. Nope. Not going to do it.

Conversation petered out. I was tired of asking questions. He was probably tired of answering them.

Literally, that was it. I was so very disappointed thinking that dating was going to be hell if they were all this boring. I took myself home when it was still light out.

Look, I'm single. I know it can happen to any of us at any time. And I've asked some of the guys why they were single. I didn't think this one was a mystery. Nothing in life satisfied him. I could only imagine he found similar flaws in every woman who crossed his path. I'd kind of like to know what my flaw was and kind of not.

When I got home, I locked my front and back doors, ate some salad, and got comfy in my pajamas.

Snuggled into bed with my Kindle and read *Thirsty* by Mia Hopkins. Great book. Can't recommend it enough. That hero wouldn't have been boring or late.

THREE

The Friends with Benefits

JANUARY 25.

I WAS SWIPING, I was dating, but I had no idea what in the hell I wanted. I was finding that all the guys I'd matched with on Bumble liked...texting.

I offered to meet in person more than once. They offered more texting. It's not that I don't love writing and putting together the story of my life, but writing is my day job. I didn't have time to have my phone in my hand day and night. With Screen Time enabled, it was becoming obvious I'd gone from one to two plus hours daily staring at my phone and not into the eyes of real people. That wasn't a good thing.

When FWB guy popped up on OKCupid, I swiped because he was cute. Even though Bumble was the only app where women *had* to initiate contact, I was tired of waiting for guys to hit me up. So I went first this time. On his profile, FWB had mentioned he was recently separated. It was something I could totally relate to.

Me: Recently separated myself. What do you like to do for fun?
FWB: Hello am sorry to hear that. I like to go the

movies, concerts, dinner, travel, go different pubs.
Yourself? Nice to meet you.

Pubs? I wanted to tell him he might be on the wrong conti-
nent or maybe there were a bunch of pubs in Los Angeles and
I'd missed them.

Me: I love theater (leaving in a moment for a play),
museums, having a glass of wine out. I work at home so
I do like to go out...I also travel quite a bit for long
stretches.
FWB: Nice. What kind of work do you do?
Me: I'm a writer. Novelist. What about you?
FWB: Very cool. Am a marketing and hospitality coor-
dinator for a law firm in Century City. How's things
going for you on this app?

Everyone wanted to know how other people's experiences
were on the various apps. It's half of what guys wanted to talk
about on dates.

From my limited experience, women matched with nearly
every guy they swiped on. Why? Because the conventional
wisdom for guys was to swipe on every single woman.

This was a completely imperfect system that left me with
dozens of matches *a day* and guys complaining that women
didn't pick them. But how could we when reading profiles and
sending messages could be a full time job.

At this point, I'd have said *disappointing*, but didn't want to
bog the conversation down with negativity.

Me: I worked in CC years back in one of those twin
buildings—though I can't remember which. The
app...it's been about a week.

FWB: OK OK cool. Have you found someone to see? Am hardly ever on this app.

Guys always said that.

It was a total lie.

OKCupid at least had a little green badge next to a guy's picture when they were online. Every time I'd logged on in the past few days, FWB was online.

I'm not sure where the impulse came from where men felt compelled to say they were never on the apps. They were *always* on the apps.

Me: That was only half a thought because the valet came with my car. Interestingly meeting people in person seems difficult. Everyone I've encountered wants to text. Not an indictment—just something I didn't expect.

FWB: I don't mind meeting, coffee or drink. Am also recently separated, not looking for anything serious, just friendship and intimacy, not just a hook up.

Me: The same. I don't think I have the capacity for a big new thing. Where in LA do you live? I'm in West Hollywood.

FWB: Sounds great. I live in The Valley. We can meet soon if you're interested.

He included his 619 number.

Me: I just moved from The Valley back to where I lived before the Grove was here. I was in Studio City.

FWB: Oh OK. Am in San Fernando, moved from San Diego recently.

I gave him my number.

Me: Maybe we can meet up for coffee tomorrow.

Tomorrow never came. Or rather tomorrow came, but not a date with FWB. I turned out that his San Fernando Valley was actually the city of San Fernando. Even after more than a decade and a half in Los Angeles, I'd never been there. I think it was the city Michael Connelley's Bosch was working in post LAPD retirement, but other than that, it was a mystery.

I Googled the location, and it turned out to be seventeen miles from West Hollywood. In Southern California time that may as well have been a million miles away. It was easily a thirty minute drive on a good traffic day. We rarely had good traffic days.

I'd offered to meet him on a late Saturday morning at a coffee shop on Santa Monica and Fairfax across the street from Starbucks. It was quieter with arguably better coffee. But he'd texted and said that he had some stuff to take care of. It was only when my phone's text tone dinged that I realized I'd forgotten that I'd set up another date for that afternoon. So I left the date and time open because the other guy (Mr. Basketball) was arguably cuter.

FWB worked in Century City near a very large mall. Like I'd texted earlier, I'd worked there myself many years back when I was doing temporary office work to help support my writing. I proposed meeting there. I figured that would provide a natural time limit if I should need an escape route.

When driving over during the middle of the day, I regretted not meeting in West Hollywood. The drive through Beverly Hills to the mall was a slow midday crawl. Because I'd walked to the mall when I'd worked across the street, I'd forgotten the serpentine parking situation.

As much of a time freak as I was, being late drove me crazy. Eventually I found a space then wove my way back through the lot, up the escalators and through the mall to Randy's Donuts. Even with my parking situation, I arrived before he did, but he was the first date to arrive on time.

He was probably six feet tall easily, and younger than me by a few years, but he wasn't as cute as his picture. Instead, he was the picture of corporate marketing, not exactly my type. I wasn't seventeen though, and still believed that attraction could grow and didn't always need to be there at the beginning. Okay, maybe I didn't believe that exactly, but I was willing to entertain the idea. Although I did wonder how many people we could or would be attracted to immediately upon meeting them.

Anyway, I switched it up and ordered chamomile tea instead of peppermint. He got coffee of some sort. He paid, though I offered to cover myself.

We found a place to sit on one of the oversized couches that dotted the common areas of the mall.

"Tell me a little bit about yourself," I said.

"I'm working for a law firm, managing marketing. I used to work in the San Diego office but can now work here."

"Are you from California?" I asked. So many of the guys on the app were native. I wasn't sure how I felt about that. Being from the east coast gave me a certain perspective on life that I didn't always share with natives. My east coast friends who'd dated and married natives complained a lot about the differences. Three thousand miles was a lot to bridge.

"San Fernando, actually," he said.

"What brought you to San Diego then?"

"I was married. Am married. Separated. I actually spend every other weekend down there now with my daughter."

"How old is she?"

"Only one. That's all the time I could get with her."

"So you drive down to San Diego."

"Every other weekend."

"If your daughter's down there, why come back?"

"My dad was sick, and my mother's not well enough to care for him. So I'm living in their garage apartment while I help them out."

"That's admirable, all that you're doing," I hedged. We were at that age. All of my friends, actually, were at the phase of life where we were so-called sandwiched between young children, or at least children who weren't self-sufficient, and parents who were facing all sorts of illnesses and needed care, often alone—widowed or divorced—or with spouses incapable of helping with sickness or care.

It was becoming obvious why he wasn't ready for any kind of serious relationship. He already had three nearly full time commitments.

"So what are you looking for?" It was becoming my new default question, one I was asking earlier and earlier. What people wrote on their profiles seemed to have little relationship (pun intended) to what they wanted.

"Intimacy." He paused, and I let it sit there a second. "I'd like to go out to dinner. Listen to live music, maybe then have sex."

I looked around as if it mattered who might be listening. Everyone said they valued honesty, but maybe Americans valued subtlety more. At least I was starting to think that I might.

Despite the shock or whatever the emotion was that made me a little bit squirmy, it was, I thought, exactly what I was looking for. But maybe not in his particular package. My unarticulated rejection felt arbitrary and a bit mean. That was the dating game, though, like fishing lots of casting, lots of culling.

Eventually I nodded. "Sounds good. I like the same kinds of things, but theater as well. That's important to me."

"So it sounds like we're compatible, then. I certainly think you're very attractive."

For some reason, people talking about my looks made me uncomfortable. In my estimation, I was a reasonably attractive woman who looked younger than her age. Gray hair and middle age weight were creeping up on me, though.

Vanity kept me exercising, waxing, getting expensive hair extensions, and dressing for my body type. I made an effort to put forward the best me that I could, though I didn't necessarily want to be complimented on the effort.

"I should let you get back to work," I said. "I certainly need to get some more words down today."

"You'll think about it? My proposal?"

I nodded in a way that I hoped looked thoughtful.

"I'll think about it."

We hugged and said our goodbyes.

I did think about it for the ten minutes it took me to weave my way through Macy's ignoring the shoes and jewelry, descending to the underground parking, and getting into my car. The relationship sounded like exactly what I wanted. Just not with him. He wasn't enough my type. A few hours later, I got this text:

FWB: It was great meeting you @Randy's Donuts.
Me: That's a heck of a shop name LOL.
FWB: I think we'd have great chemistry, Jolie.

Then a few days later, another text arrived. It was his Hail Mary pass.

FWB: Will you let me know your thoughts on my proposition.

Me: Friends with benefits, right?
FWB: Yes, I'm looking for intimacy with no strings...
Think it over and get back to me. Have a lovely night.

I didn't get back to him. Honestly, it seemed like his life was full. An almost toddler a four-hour drive away, needy parents, a demanding job. I let silence be my answer.

FOUR

Mr. Basketball

JANUARY 20.

THE REASON I pushed back the date with FWB was for this guy.

Mr. Basketball took a good picture. He'd posted a bunch of great ones on Tinder, and I was all in. While I was in the middle of texting with FWB, I got a text from this guy.

Mr. Basketball: I'm almost done with my work in Culver City. Can we meet at 1 near your place?

So I put FWB off and agreed to meet with Mr. Basketball. This time it was a coffee shop near me. Guys were willing to travel to me for dates. I took advantage of that.

He was standing outside the place when I walked up to the front door. The hug hello was awkward. I wasn't sure if it was because we were awkward with each other or because he was somewhere north of six feet tall. Any inches past five foot eleven was a lot for me.

We walked into the industrial space that housed the coffee shop. It was all cement floors, exposed iron beams, and austere wood furniture. I think this was far outside Mr. Basketball's usual. He hesitated a long time before ordering a fresh pressed juice that was well north of five dollars.

I had jasmine tea. This wasn't the kind of place to serve something as lowbrow as mint. It was the kind of place that roasted their own beans and only made pour over coffee. I'm not a coffee connoisseur by any means so this didn't mean much to me.

My days of having my own espresso machine, bean grinder, or even a coffee maker were long over. My ex had two main complaints. One was that coffee gave him heartburn. The second was that I was a crap wife for not making him regular coffee in the mornings along with the scratch breakfast I made seven days a week. Clearly that was a game I couldn't win, so I'd stopped playing.

Juice in hand, he lowered himself to one of the metal stools. Instead of sitting across a wide expanse of wood and steel, I perched on the stool so that we were at the corner, next to each other.

"What were you doing in Culver City?" I asked.

"Taking the last of my physical therapist qualification exams," he answered.

"Wow, okay. Changing careers?"

"Yeah. It's about time. I needed something different."

"Where do you live, then?"

"Pasadena. With my sister. We inherited the house from my dad."

Another California native, I guessed. I winced inwardly, because I just didn't get these guys. But I was here, he was cute, compelling green eyes. I skirted the issue of his father. It turned out that lots of us had fathers who died. It could be a touchy subject, not first date material.

"Pasadena to Culver City. That's not the best drive." Damn I should be banished to boring conversation hell for that one. I couldn't think of what to ask him, though. I wasn't one to be tongue tied. Maybe I'd already run out of casual conversation during my first couple of dates.

"Have you ever had one of those DNA tests?" he asked out of the blue.

My mind scrambled at the change in conversation. DNA?

"My parents are my parents," I started. "I'm sure of that, so no, I don't think so."

"Not that kind. The genetic kind."

My mind scattered again as I tried to pick up the pieces of the puzzle I was clearly missing.

"Oh, do you mean Twenty-three and Me? Sure I've done that." I had because I wanted to know if my genetic makeup fit with my fairly well documented family history. Indeed it did. The African, Native American, and European percentages were in line with family lore.

"Me too. My father is black," he said.

All became clear right then. Mr. Basketball was really light. Very pale, actually. Most people would probably assume he was white. I hadn't thought anything about his genetic makeup because I didn't think that way. I'm not one of those people who will ever say I don't see race, because that's not true.

In Southern California, though, there are so many people who are a mix of many different things, that I never really make any presumptions about their background. I don't care as that's not a criteria in dating. Cute and long hair factor in my computations far more than their makeup.

I'm not naïve, though. I knew that what he was saying was probably of monumental importance to some people, so he was right to get out in front of that. I just wish he'd thought of a less awkward way to say it. Or at least some way that hadn't left me scrambling for clues. I'd seen other guys like him list their race and preferences for the race of their future partner right on their profiles.

"Okay," I said. Then I changed the subject. He would have

to make his own assumptions about my genealogy from my looks. I really didn't want to get into my family's own melting pot of a background.

"What did you do before you decided to become a physical therapist?" I asked.

"Basketball. I played in high school, then college, then coached. I'm done with it, though."

I sat and sipped, somewhat relieved. Maybe the hug had been awkward because he *was* tall.

"Your height?"

"I'm six foot five," he said.

"That's a full fifteen inches taller than me," I said.

"I'm taller than a lot of people. My daughter is getting pretty tall as well."

Kids.

He had one.

This was something that I thought people should put on their profile. He hadn't. I'd tried to share everything that I thought was important with my own. I'd worked a good few hours on it before I finalized it and uploaded it to the three apps.

This is mine:

Full time writer of romance. Part time jet setter. Lover of live theater. Single mom of a nine-year-old. Short and curvy. Looking for someone who enjoys dinner (in or out), theater, and what comes after. Swipe left if you don't like kissing.

It, along with a three-week-old headshot as well as shots of me on my last vacation in Greece were what I'd uploaded. No old pictures. No hiding that I had a kid. No bull.

I believed honesty to be the best policy. Let's just say not everyone agreed. I had to work with what men were willing to share, though.

"How old is your daughter?" I asked. I had my own child

and had zero Brady Bunch type fantasies. I wasn't looking for someone to help me raise my son.

One father was enough.

My dating time was severely limited to two or three days a week, and I wanted to be upfront about that. Also, any guy I met was not going to be the top priority in my life, ever.

That said, I did want to know their relationship to their own child or children. I thought it probably said a lot about them. What, I wasn't sure. I collected the information, though, and fit it in with the rest of what they said about themselves to make my own judgment.

"Thirteen going on twenty," he said. "She lives with her mom. All she wants from me are rides to her friends' houses and for me to pay her phone bill."

Now that sounded like there was more to the story, but I wouldn't press. Not on a first date.

"Sounds typical. My son still thinks I hang the moon, so I'm holding on to that," I said.

"You should as long as you can."

Mr. Basketball was a perfectly lovely guy. This date wasn't going anywhere, though. We finished our drinks, and I walked him back to his car. He wanted to get on the road before traffic got crazy. I got it. Pasadena was a place I hardly ever went because the drive was less than enjoyable from my part of the southland.

We hugged when we got to his car. Then he offered to walk me past his car, to my house a few blocks farther north.

"If you'd like to get together another time, for dinner or something, I'd like that," he said.

"Sure." He was really cute so that tipped the scales toward a likely second date. Maybe it would be more interesting than the first.

"I'll give you my number," he offered. I put it into my phone.

"Would you want to invite me up?" he asked. Then laughed it off like a huge joke. He leaned down and gave me a second hug, a kiss on the cheek, and turned back toward his car with a wave.

Honestly, I'd thought the same since I was clearly not a prude. Something about him, though, said that he'd have said, 'no' and judged me for it. Or he'd have said, 'yes' and judged me harshly for it. I'd discarded the thought before it had come out of my mouth, though, when he'd mentioned a second date.

Since I was already home, I walked upstairs to my apartment. So that he had my number, I sent a text about an hour later.

Me: Great meeting you today. Thanks for the tea and conversation. Hope the drive home wasn't too bad.
Let's talk soon.
Mr. Basketball: Likewise, no the drive wasn't too bad.

Neither of us texted again. One day when I was on Tinder, I scrolled through my matches to find he'd unmatched. It wasn't great for either of us, I guess.

They say you have to kiss a bunch of frogs before you meet a prince. I was neither sad nor happy about this lack of connection. More resolved to go ahead and hope that there was someone out there for me.

FIVE

Justin Time

FEBRUARY 1.

THERE WAS something about a Friday afternoon that had been getting me down since the divorce. I didn't know precisely what it was, but this one had me all hot and bothered without the prospect of a date on the horizon. I'd been swiping and texting, but I hadn't found someone I wanted to meet in person on this night.

The upside and downside of online dating were the same—hookup culture. Sometimes I wanted a serious conversation and I got a dick pic. Sometimes I wanted a hookup and I got a guy who wanted to get to know me. I swear there should be completely separate apps for exactly what you're looking for.

It's almost that way...but not quite. Plus guys say they want one thing and really want another. I think many of them put relationship because that would pull the most matches. Them, I mostly avoided. It was the guys who put casual, non-monogamous and one night stand in their profile, who then texted about long term relationships and marriage who were a mystery.

It was about one in the afternoon when I started scrolling through my history looking for someone I could meet for a hookup. I tried Drummer Boy, first because a known quantity was better than an unknown one. He texted back that his relationship status had moved from single to complicated.

That was something I didn't want to touch with a ten foot pole. I just hoped that he had been truthful about being single on the night we met because I had zero desire for drama or to have been the reason some woman was pulling her hair out with jealousy or worry.

Between the three apps, I was sure there had been some very blatant come-ons. There were two. I opted out of the first guy, because he was still in his twenties. Great stamina, maybe. Had grown up with porn, probably. I wasn't ready to tackle someone who might think sex was all performance.

Fortunately, I had an offer in my OKCupid history from a week earlier. I thought it was time to pull the trigger on that one.

Justin Time: I'd love to meet you.
Me: I do love meeting new people...tell me a little about yourself.
Justin Time: I'm just a normal guy. I work for different temp services. I'd love to fill your pussy today if you're free.
Me: Alas, I'm busy for exactly one week... but if you're game later we should meet up.
Justin: I would definitely love to meet up when you're free. I'd like to slide my hard cock deep in your pussy as soon as we meet.

Feb 1. 12:58pm

Me: I think it's time to chat...
Justin Time: Let me know when you can meet. I'd

like to slide my hard cock in your pussy as soon as we meet. We can chat and say hello while my cock pumps in and out of your pussy. Let me know when you can meet and where.

Me: I'm having the kind of day where I think you may be able to solve at least one of my immediate problems....Text me to talk possible logistics...

Ready to get off the app, I gave him my phone number.

His first text to me was a current selfie. He was still cute. The next was a dick pic. I wasn't sure I'd asked for that, but at least there was no mystery as to what I'd be getting.

Justin Time: Hi, this is me from OKC. I hope you can ride my hard cock soon.

Me: Well there. (That was in response to the erect penis). What's your schedule like today?

Justin Time: I'm pretty free today, but I don't have a car. Do you live close to 3rd and Western?

Me: Fairly close. I'm in West Hollywood.

Justin Time: I can prolly come over and slide in your pussy if you're free right now. I hope I can cum in you.

Me: I'll be free in a few. Any issues with condoms?

I was free then, but I was building in time to back out. When I'd met Drummer Boy for dinner, I hadn't decided until we were kissing by my car that I was going to have sex with him. Without the buffer of wine and time, I was making a decision based solely on a photo and sexy chat.

Justin Time: I can wear a condom. Do you have any? What's your address? I'll get in the shower then come over.

I was panicking a tiny bit. This had to fall under the category of zero vetting.

Me: Smoker? Checking on my deal breakers.
Justin Time: Not a smoker.
Me: I have condoms.
Justin Time: OK address. I'll get in the shower now and get ready to come over to your place.

My mind was in two different places. One was horny. The other was reviewing all the scenarios where I invite a guy to come to my place and he cuts me up into tiny pieces and someone has to explain to my friends and family the stupidity of my death, which would have been prevented if I just reached for the vibrator in the back of the drawer of my bedside table instead of my phone.

Me: No batshit crazy kinks?
Justin Time: Nope. Just like to walk in and see your pussy spread open ready for a hard cock. I do like cuckold so I hope you've been riding some other hard cocks recently.

And that was it. I texted my address. He took an Uber. He arrived in ten minutes. Los Angeles isn't so big and traffic filled when you need it to be.

A few months ago, I read this book called, *Come as You Are: The Surprising New Science that Will Transform Your Sex Life.* I'm not sure it transformed my sex life. Not the nonexistent one my ex-husband and I didn't have. But the book was eye opening. It talked about how every woman's sexual response was different. I think she said more or less that we all have the same parts. They're just organized differently on every single woman.

For me orgasms have always been easy. Reading a sexy romance can get me aroused. A man touching me just about anywhere has the same effect. Even thinking about it works as well.

When Justin Time knocked on the door, I was more than halfway there. I opened the door. He came in and closed it behind me, then pushed me up against the wood and kissed me. He simultaneously kicked off his shoes and shoved one hand under my bra, then the other went into my pants.

"You're already wet for me," he whispered when his finger slipped inside me.

I was.

In less than a minute we were naked and into my bedroom. I'd drawn the shades, but it was light enough to see him. Justin Time lived up to all his talk. In ten minutes, I came once. When he entered me, it wasn't more than a few minutes before I came again.

After he came, he collapsed on the other side of my bed trying to get his breathing under control.

"You write music?" I asked a little curious about this man I'd just let into my body.

"Commercial jingles," he said. "I'm only working part time. Mostly living off royalties."

"And you live in Koreatown?"

"My mom's Japanese, he said. My dad's white. I grew up in Iowa, but moved here right after college. I really like Koreatown."

"It's a great neighborhood."

"I gotta go," he said. He searched around the room for his clothes. "I'm taking care of my ex-girlfriend's cat. I've gotta get to Los Feliz before the traffic gets bad so I can feed him."

"Nice meeting you." It was the best I could come up with. I put on my robe and showed him out.

Being with him had done exactly what I'd wanted it to do.

It had made me feel wanted. It had satisfied my craving for sex. It had taken my mind off all my problems. After, I made myself dinner, had a glass of wine, and binged watched Netflix. It couldn't have been a better night.

Right before I settled into bed for the night, there was a text from him.

Justin Time: It was good to see you. You made my cock so hard, I hope I can cum in you again.
Me: You made my afternoon a lot better.

That last was the absolute truth.

SIX

I Blame it on Reddit - 99 Books

FEBRUARY 2.

I BLAME Reddit for this date. I was surfing OKCupid and got that usual notification about someone liking me. I clicked over and there was a new guy. He was an actor who loved to read and, though not the cutest, was quite pleasant looking. But there was a single fact that stopped me. He listed his height at five foot four inches tall.

I'm not a height queen. I'm short, so it doesn't much matter to me. My main issue is that I really don't want to outweigh them, so slight guys aren't for me. 99 Books wasn't slight, but he was short.

Before starting this little dating project, Reddit wasn't something I ever read. But I was Googling whether the guys on Bumble will ever meet in person and came upon a thread titled 'Gentlemen under 6'o'" about dating and height.

Of course lots of men both over and under six feet made lots of comments about how women are far more particular on dating apps than they are in real life. Like any woman with an ounce of compassion and empathy, I started feeling quite shallow myself. I made a comment on the 'Gentlemen under

6'0'" thread about having a few things in common with a short guy but not swiping right.

That was followed by an immediate 'ouch' comment from another guy. I read further down how guys—who said they were otherwise perfectly fine—were often if not mostly over-looked if they were five foot eight or under. Ouch was right.

Sufficiently induced by guilt, I went back to the app and swiped right.

His first message to me was probably a heavy dose of fore-shadowing.

> **99 Books:** There is one thing that I'm not thrilled
> with in regards to dating. I have a roommate
> temporarily. As an artist, I'm sure you might
> understand.
> **Me:** I hope that's not too stressful.

Because for me a roommate would be stressful. Introvert plus the potential of someone being messy stresses me out. My last roommate was my ex-husband. The fact that he felt like an annoying roommate was probably a huge problem in and of itself. Which was why I was single...and dating.

> **99 Books:** Only when I lose a chance to date someone
> I'm interested in.

Since I live alone roommates weren't a big issue. Though I could see how it would be awkward hanging out at some guy's house—because all the advice is that you have to at least see a guy's house to make sure he's single, not crazy, not homeless, etcetera, etcetera—with someone else there. Especially after a certain age. But Southern California is expensive, so I was trying to be more generous. I'm gathering financial security

wasn't one of 99 Books traits, but for now, that wasn't important to me. I was happily supporting myself. I wasn't looking
for anyone to support me.

I was looking for a friend for dinner, for theater, for intimacy like FWB guy had summarized. This wasn't a search for a
billionaire, just for a companion. A cute one with long hair and
creativity, preferably.

Over the next couple of weekdays texting, I learned 99
Books was from Michigan and thought himself a flirty goof-
ball. He liked how I looked. That was starting to be a constant
refrain. Personally it felt like a given on a dating app, but men
really liked to mention it time and again. I don't mind a
compliment. Might even like one from the right guy at the
right time, but before I met them wasn't that great. It was
kind of superficial because I was more than how I looked.

99 Books: Do you have a type of guy you like or a list
of must haves?

Now, I made a list many pages back of my type. And 99
Books didn't fit within those narrow parameters. Every book,
person, advice giver suggested dating outside of narrow parameters because one never knew. That wasn't something I was
going to include in a text, though.

Me: Before I answer, an explanation is welcome.
Otherwise, I'll probably say random stuff that doesn't
answer you. And talking at cross purposes...
99 Books: Ok. I ask because I have been having
dating troubles and am always looking for ways to
improve. Not sure if it's me or something outside of
myself.

Nothing says confidence like a guy you haven't met in person telling you that he's got dating troubles bigger than his roommate.

Me: I'm currently (like two months) in an advice columnist obsession. One columnist insists that *you* are always the common denominator. In theory, a trusted friend will tell you the unvarnished truth if asked. That's totally unsolicited advice with me having zero knowledge. It comes with a grain of salt.

I've got a handle on my issues. But that's what therapy has been wonderful for. Also, a friend recently gave me my own unvarnished truth. It was something another friend said more than twenty years ago. I heard it better this go round, and I'll work on it or not depending on...who knows what...but I can't say someone didn't tell me.

The unvarnished truth was that I was difficult to get to know. I grew up in one of those families where no one ever talked about emotions. Everything else, sure.

Emotions, never.

Twenty years ago, I didn't care much about it. These days I could very much see how it could hold me back. I'd started practicing on friends. Trying to show my love and appreciation for the very smart women I'm happy to call my friends. Dating was the next frontier.

99 Books: But you are correct. I am the common denominator. My friends tell me to be patient and that things are turning around for me in all areas of my life. Just takes some recognition and understanding on the part of the other person. Ok. I have had some struggles but I keep fighting. I just wish someone would see that instead of the absence of. I'm a unique person. I'm intelligent, talented, polite, caring, funny, and well spoken. I have things to offer. I can be romantic...

Me: I try to look at it this way: if people give you a quick 'no' then you can move on to 'yes' quicker. I used to hate it—HATE IT— when people said that kind of thing to me. And there was a lot of that advice in a particular period of my life. But I live by it now, because changing other people's minds isn't my super power.

99 Books: Very well put. I know my life isn't perfect right now. But I stay positive. I like your vibe.

That was followed by a lot of 'good nights' and 'good mornings,' until we agreed to meet on Saturday afternoon. It would have been wine at five, but his dating problem confessional moved him up to decaf coffee at four.

99 Books: That works fine. Something relaxing. I will plan the next date should there be one. I'm sorry if it fell to you to do this time. Ok. You actually sound pretty awesome. Extraordinary. Are you a really serious person?

Me: Probably.

Lighthearted and fun were not traits that were often used to describe me.

99 Books: Ok. Well I will hopefully provide a balance. I can be serious when need be but I like to make people laugh. I will tell you more in person, but for now I will say that I am just a nice guy, who has come to a point where I don't need anyone but it would be nice to have someone. And take it a step at a time. Trying to find my piece of heaven.

I wasn't laughing yet. He next asked me had I read a book called *Infinite Jest*.

David Foster Wallace and the title's three hundred eighty-eight endnotes wasn't on my list of romance and mysteries that were my nighttime bread and <u>butter</u>. I'd let go of reading books that challenged me to stay awake and replaced them instead with books that challenged me to look at my emotions. This seemed much more important at this stage in my life. To each his own, though.

Me: What are you wearing?
99 Books: Gray pants, a black v neck and a pea coat.

I made a mental note until a new text came in.

99 Books: Actually, I will wear the nicer shirt.

Had I not rated the best shirt the first time around? I was thinking he should censor himself and run all this stuff in front of all those friends who'd maybe help him with dating.

Of course, it was raining again. This winter had been the rainiest in a long time. It was a bonus that The Grove provided golf umbrellas, so my cashmere and wool stayed dry on the walk over from the valet to the bookstore. I took myself up to the coffee shop in Barnes and Noble and while I was waiting, took a look for friends' books on the shelves. Sadly, I didn't see any. The romance shelves were woefully thin.

It may have been my first disappointment, meeting this date. He was the first who'd lied about his height. Five foot four was a stretch. He was at most my height. It was hard to tell as I was wearing boots that lifted me up an inch or two.

It was apparent immediately his problem with dating. It was as if he'd made a point to drive all this way, but not...bathe. Hair product was one thing. Greasy hair was another. He'd switched out the V-neck of whatever sort for a green plaid button up that was buttoned all the way up. And yes, he'd worn a pea coat. It was oddly ill fitting and out of place, though.

I was very familiar with the limitations of off the rack clothes. I was also familiar with the magic a ten dollar tailoring could do. I wanted that for him. But I was going to leave that up to his friends. I ordered a tea. A very small tea. I don't remember what he ordered. I was just grateful that a table opened up.

"Have you heard of the ninety-nine books challenge?" He took a sip of his drink.

I shook my head, but retrieved my phone from my purse. I didn't usually rely on gadgets on a date, but this one desperately needed Siri. She was happy to populate my screen with a three page list of a classic reads challenge.

"Are you doing this?" I asked turning the phone in his direction.

"I think I'm at the phase of my life when I want to challenge myself. I want to join Groundlings, get my acting career off the ground, and read these books.

I scrolled through the list.

"I haven't read *War and Peace*," I offered. I was satisfied to have completed the ninety-eight book challenge.

"But you've read the rest?"

I nodded. "Most in high school."

I tried to carry the conversation for another hour or so. I talked about writing romance, living in Los Angeles. Then I was exhausted. I looked at my watch. It was thirty-seven minutes after five. I stood and tossed my cup into a receptacle.

"I have to get back to work," I said.

"Let me walk you to your car."

So we walked to the valet. By my count, I'd dragged this one out thirty-seven minutes longer than necessary. I took myself home. It was going to be the second early night of the weekend, but the first had been far more satisfying. I took out my phone to text like I'd done before.

Me: Thanks for the coffee and conversation. Hope your drive back is safe.

It wasn't my best conversation ender. Though I'd not yet learned to talk about emotional stuff, I'd learned how to be polite.

99 Books: No problem. Thank you for meeting me. We will talk soon. Made it home safe. You look even better in person.

I didn't text back. I knew what was coming. In the two or three hours while I waited for that text, I had texted a friend for advice.

Me: I can't believe this. I'm well past the age when I should know this. I'm Googling how to turn a guy down for a second date.
Friend: You have to be direct.

When his text came, I was ready.

99 Books: Hi Jolie. How was your day? I may be breaking some unwritten rule but I don't care. Can I see you again?

I didn't know there were rules or which ones may be broken. But I took my friends advice and a bit of Google's.

> **Me:** No rules broken. It was great meeting you Saturday but I'm not interested in another date.

SEVEN

Thunderbolt

JANUARY 22.

HAVE YOU HEARD OF BUMBLE?

No?

Let me tell you, this dating app is a pressure cooker. Once you match with a guy, you have twenty-four hours to make the first move. Everyone who knew anything about dating apps promised me that Bumble was the place to start.

It was supposed to be chock full of guys who were looking for more than a hookup. The app supposedly banned naked chest pics. It was supposed to be low on the kind of guys who would send dick pics.

Look, I'm not gonna lie. I like a nice penis as much as the next girl. But if I don't know you, I don't really want to see yours. Initially the app didn't disappoint. Right out of the gate, I swiped right and matched with some pretty hot guys. Conversations were smart, funny, and interesting. There was one huge flaw.

None of them wanted to meet in person.

I don't mind texting, I guess. But I have this full time job, you know, writing romance, a nearly full time son, and other stuff to do. The last thing I wanted to do was text all day and night. I got on dating apps to meet people in the real world not to boost my ego via sexy chat.

After the first few let downs, I felt burned out. So when Thunderbolt and I matched, I let it expire. He was super cute and honestly, I couldn't think of a thing to say that would be interesting enough to get a response from him.

Ladies, I think I have a much greater appreciation for guys after being on this app because thinking of a good opener is harder than I thought.

After my disappointment with Bumble I signed up for OKCupid and Tinder. Yes, they were known for being hookup apps. But once I was truly honest with myself, I was thinking that I could do with a few good hookups until I found someone I wanted to meet more than once.

OKCupid had brought me Drummer Boy and Justin Time. I'd been afraid of Tinder. I wasn't sure I could move fast enough for an app where guys wanted to meet you that night.

But one lonely (and if I'm honest—horny) night I was swiping on Tinder and there was Thunderbolt. He was still hella cute. I swiped right and we matched because he'd already swiped right on me.

My takeaway: he'd picked me twice. The universe was telling me something. I did not hesitate the second time around.

A few weeks had made me bolder, so I texted him first through the app.

Me: I feel like we've done this dance before...on a different app...Still think you're amazingly handsome.
Thunderbolt: What a lovely thing to say.
Me: It's true. If you ever want to meet up LMK.
Thunderbolt: Sounds fun working late tonight.

He was busy. There was more, but basically I gave him my

number and who knew what I did next. That was a Saturday at ten o'clock at night. I didn't think much more of it.

Then Tuesday, right when I was about to tuck myself in bed at nine thirty because I had a spin class early the next morning, I got a text.

Thunderbolt: Hey, it's me from the wonderful world of Tinder.
Me: Oh, hey there. Tinder is either wonderful or truly will end mankind. I'm leaning toward it being a good thing.
Thunderbolt: Just depends on the day. Maybe both. Working like mad but could use a break. How about tonight, meetup?
Me: I'm having a debate in my head as I have to get up at the ass crack of dawn tomorrow and I'm wondering *how* awake I need to be...
Thunderbolt: So why don't I stop by? We can have fun, but be efficient, Jolie.

Because I'd been getting into my jammies and considering which book boyfriend I was going to take to bed with me, I hadn't been by my phone for a good twenty minute. It was, I'd say, about 9:30 by the time I saw that text. And let me say, I was surprised.

Three days after matching with him, I was about to get what I wanted served straight up. I swear I thought we'd reached the peak of civilization when I learned that I could put my thumb on my phone and get takeout. Now I was putting my thumb on my phone and finding really cute men who wanted to have sex. It's a bit surreal to say the least.

My hands shook. I couldn't think what in the hell to say, then I typed the text above. Right at that moment, nothing sounded better than efficient fun.

Half hour later, there he was at my front door, delivered via Uber. He was even better looking than his pictures. It was like staring straight into the sun.

I've always prided myself on being the 'cool girl' when dating. I rarely let my guard down. Instead, I have this persona that makes me into a girl they can't resist. It works well, sometimes too well.

The chemistry was immediate and I really didn't have it in me to be the cool girl. Instead, I was the weird girl.

Because one of my biggest fantasies had become reality.

I have a couple of fantasies that roll around in my head from time to time. One involves a sexy photographer. The other a documentary film maker. I shit you not. So when Thunderbolt takes a seat at my kitchen counter, bottle of Malbec in hand, and starts describing the work he needs a break from, I nearly shit my pants. He was about to premier his first documentary feature film at a festival in a month and a half.

And those pants were yoga pants because after my shower, I couldn't for the life of me figure out what in the hell one wears for a Tinder hookup.

Lingerie?

I didn't own any and even if I did, satin and lace was so 1970s soap opera.

Nothing? Answering my door wrapped in a bathrobe seemed presumptuous and well a lot weird. So I'd settled on some Lululemon black leggings and an Old Navy T-shirt. This was the winning combo I was wearing while standing in my kitchen, my back to my farmhouse sink, freaking the fuck out.

Thunderbolt brandished the bottle of Malbec he'd brought.

"Wine?"

I couldn't imagine adding wine to my nervous stomach.

"No." I shook my head.

"Sure?"

"I'm very sure."

He held up his hands. "I'm not an alcoholic. So I'm good."

I asked him a bit about the film he was working on. He told me about the film that he was in the final stages of editing that was going to tour on the festival circuit.

While I was asking something about film editing, or story-telling, or something, he stepped down from the stool and walked around from the dining room side to the kitchen side of my breakfast bar. In just seconds, he was standing in front of me. He slipped a hand along my cheek.

"Gotta break the ice," he said. Then he kissed me. It was a good kiss. A kiss that said there was a lot of potential for what was coming next.

I offered him a glass of water because I needed one for myself because my throat was closed with nerves. I gave him a glass and somehow he got water all over himself and the floor and most definitely not in the glass.

That more than the kiss really broke the ice. I got one of my favorite fire engine red dish towels and mopped up the mess. Then I took his free hand, the one that wasn't holding a glass of ice water, and led him to my bedroom.

"This is a great apartment," he said as he backed into my bedroom. "Amazingly neat."

This was not the conversation I wanted to have. But I played along for a moment.

"Where do you live?"

"Rent control studio not far from here."

Like nearly every apartment in West Hollywood of a certain vintage, mine was rent control as well, but I didn't want to talk about stabilization laws.

So I stopped talking and pulled him closer because I wanted more kissing. When I'd been a teenager in the first throes of heady love all my college boyfriend and I had done

JOLIE MOORE

was kiss. It felt like we'd passed hours that way. At seventeen, I thought that the kinds of feelings women had in the romance novels I devoured were finally mine. Unfortunately, I married someone who didn't like kissing me. I was determined to make up for lost time.

Thunderbolt was no slouch at kissing or touching or any of the elements of foreplay that I'd sorely missed. And he was efficient. In no time, he was fisting himself and ready to enter me. Like Drummer Boy before him, I had to stop right in the middle.

"Do you have a condom?" It was both a stupid question and not. Obviously, I didn't think he'd pull one out of thin air.

"No? You?"

"*Oh, my God.* Yes. Gimme a sec."

I opened my bra drawer and dug through, looking for the little pink foil packets. But I had neither contacts nor glasses and for the life of me couldn't find them in the sea of black silk, nylon, and poking underwires.

"You've gotta do this. I'm blind here." I threw that over my shoulder

He had better eyes than me and pulled the only two condoms from the drawer and tossed them on the nightstand. Then he whispered.

Yep, a man who had a full voice only moments before whispered what he wanted during sex. I wanted to ask him to speak up, but I spent most of the time trying to hear what he wanted: me on hands and knees, me on my side, or whatever it was.

He paused at some point and held his breath.

"You're really tight."

"I like to think of it as a feature, not a flaw."

It was a feature that worked for both of us, because in a few minutes we both came. He went to my bathroom to get rid of the condom. I lay on my bed. He came back and lay next to me, still breathing pretty heavily.

As Thunderbolt's breathing slowed, I asked the one question I knew I shouldn't, but curiosity got the better of me.

"Why are you single?"

"I'm waiting for the one," he said.

"The one?"

"I've had girlfriends. I've even lived with someone for a few years. I'm waiting to meet someone and get hit by a thunderbolt so I know that we're meant to be."

I may have actually uttered, 'awwww' out loud. It seemed both naïve, and quaint, and romantic all at the same time.

"What are you doing in the meantime?" I asked.

He patted my naked ass. "Tinder. And I get massages."

The conversation that came after was an education for me. I'd heard of 'happy endings,' and so-called 'jack shacks.' Thunderbolt had been to them all. He had a place he loved the best in Pasadena. The conversation actually morphed to real massages. He liked to get them weekly to relieve the stress and tension of movie editing and being hunched over a computer for hours a day.

"You should do them," he said. "You need to get loose baby."

Then he was kissing me again and rolling on the second condom. I wanted to pause and tell him that he should tell a girl that he had a twenty minute refractory period. I guess he knew that he'd need both condoms. I'd only bought three when I was thinking about dating, and now I was completely out. I'd have to remedy that.

EIGHT

The Amazing Date

FEBRUARY 8.

ON SUPER BOWL SUNDAY, I wasn't watching the Super Bowl. I actually don't quite remember what I was doing.

Maybe writing.

Maybe reading.

Maybe not much of anything.

But like other days when I found myself with a few minutes on my hands, I went swiping on Tinder. Like I'd said to Thunderbolt, this app was either the best idea ever or the beginning of the downfall of Western Civilization. Believe it or not, I'm still not sure. Although to be honest, it's probably a bit of both.

Anyway, some Sunday when my neighborhood was full of cheering, I was swiping. As usual, a cute guy popped up. I've already given you the parameters of my type. He was numbers one and two. He fit into it to a 'T.' Super cute. Long hair. His bio promised he was laid back with no drama or issues. After years of nothing but drama and issues, I'm learning to love a life that's drama free.

So I swiped and matched and messaged. Weird thing is that Bumble is not the only app where you have to message first. I've heard that on Tinder, it's full of guys messaging you. They swipe on me, but rarely message me. And when I initiate, they always say I was too pretty to message.

Newsflash: Pretty girls want to date too.

Anyway, this guy—I'm going to call him Classic Car for reasons that will become obvious later—replied.

He was also *not* watching the Super Bowl. He was born and raised in Southern California. It's a thing. Not everyone is a transplant. I usually go for East Coast guys. But that didn't turn out to be a good decision many times over, so I was willing to branch out.

There are a lot of conversations I have on apps, but there was something about this guy that got to me. Maybe it was that we'd both gone to Catholic school and had both been in constant trouble for talking.

Or maybe it was that he loved traveling as much as I did. He'd just gotten back from a trip. It was probably the story he told about the one time he'd tried being in a band. His friend had gotten him a little bit drunk and next thing he knew, he was fronting their band and covering The Doors before a live audience.

Something about that was both endearing and vulnerable. It hooked me like a fish. Or it was that he was super cute with long hair. It was probably that last thing as shallow as that was.

Either way next thing I knew I was giving him my number. Let me tell you something...this guy has mastered the texting game. He's not the smoothest with words, but he was good. Every morning there was a 'good morning' text, usually in Spanish. Every night there was a good night text. And in between? Little, funny doses of his daily life.

He buys and refurbishes old cars. He still had his first car, a 1966 Plymouth Sport Fury. He'd just spent some time in Mexico. He liked jazz standards. So I was super excited to see him on Friday.

It was the first date that I was really looking forward to. I wish I could pinpoint what it was that got me, because my friends have asked more than once.

I still can't answer. He was cute, he had long hair, he took a mean selfie, and he knew his way around a text. Unlike nearly every other person I'd swiped right on, he wasn't an artist, or singer, or documentary film maker, though.

He was in sales of all things.

Every time I've told friends that, they've frowned in complete misunderstanding. But he's not painting or writing or tortured, they'd ask. I'd shake my head and produce a Mona Lisa smile because I didn't have an answer. Although I was starting to think that maybe I had enough of the tortured artist in me for the both of us.

Friday came all too quickly. We'd agreed to meet at Harlowe, a huge bar in West Hollywood—my stomping grounds. He lives far out in the San Gabriel Valley, the home of cities like Pasadena, El Monte, and San Marino and probably a whole long list of others I don't know the names of. Everyone said you should only date people who live close by. Thunderbolt insisted on a two or three mile radius. But I was willing to bend that rule, especially if he was willing to drive.

I have this game I play with myself. Before each date, I decide what kind of girl I'm going to be. The answer usually pivots between 'hot girl' and 'cool girl.'

In a different life, I'd probably have loved being 'manic pixie girl,' but don't now, and probably didn't then, have the ability to manifest that energy and carry it off. And I'd burned through too many years of geeky but cute 'smart girl,' and was ready to leave that one behind.

That night I had landed on cool girl. I got there early, handed over my card to run a tab, and got a pinot to keep me company. In the meantime, I texted with my guy friend and downstairs neighbor about sex and dating in LA. He's been divorced four years longer than I and has more answers than questions.

I alternated between texting him, flirting with a different guy on OKCupid who kept promising to come and 'take care of' any creepy guys who bothered me, and my Kindle, but honestly none of it could keep my attention.

I was nervous. Freaking nervous. I hadn't been nervous since forever. Instead, I watched my pinot disappear into my jiggling leg. When it trilled, I lifted my phone, and this time the text was from my date. He was a couple of minutes out...parking.

Me: What are you wearing?
Classic Car: My birthday suit. (Pause. I watched the gray dots pulse). That was a joke. Sport coat.
Classic Car: Blue jeans. Cowboy boots. Long hair.

He was true to his word. He'd actually made an effort, so I was thrilled to stand up from the leather chair I'd been sitting in for far too long and hug him.

Yes, girl, he smelled so good. Broad shoulders, great scarf, better hair. Since I couldn't sex him up right there, though trust me, I thought about it, I backed away and returned to my chair.

He sat on another chair catty-corner from me.

He ordered a beer of some kind after consulting with the server. I have zero idea about beer and am not adding it to my list of things to learn more about. I had a second pinot.

After an hour or so, his face got all serious.

"You have kids?"

"One son. He's nine. I'll show you a picture." Like most moms I imagine, I have a million pictures of my kid on my iPhone. Some of those are weird selfies that my son can take without unlocking the phone. So I showed him the latest, my son smiling while daydreaming in my dining room.

"I have two," he said. For some reason that surprised me. Again, it wasn't in his very slim profile. He showed me pictures of his one-year-old son and three year old daughter. We talked about kids for a bit. I mentioned that I didn't have my kid on weekends. He didn't say anything about his own custody schedule. It seemed intrusive to ask.

More wine came. Fortunately, he'd ordered food and more importantly water as well.

Then we talked—for another three hours. About what, I couldn't tell you. He was smart and funny and humble and interesting.

Then West Hollywood late night life happened. What do I mean? Well, it went from cool adults in their thirties drinking and laughing and eating bar food, to half naked twenty-one-year-olds. When the host asked us to stand so they could take out the furniture, I figured that was our cue.

Did I mention I was nervous and holding up the cool girl façade was taking all of my energy? Did I mention that California wines are hugely alcoholic? Did I mention my third drink—yeah I'm only five foot two—that my third drink was a Long Island Iced tea? I was able to stand and get on my suede jacket only with a massive dose of concentration.

Getting into his sedan for that two-block ride home. That...that was a challenge. I chalked it up to the fact that I have an SUV, and am accustomed to stepping up into a car rather than sitting down in one. That would have been a lie.

It was because I'd gone from 'cool girl' to 'drinky girl' in a matter of hours and holding my liquor was all I could do. Not walk or talk, but hold my damned liquor so I didn't really embarrass myself or ruin the upholstery in his Nissan.

We drove the few blocks to my place, and he pulled behind my building. At least that was something I could do, direct him down the driveway and into the parking by my back door. Thank God, he had manners or chivalry or a good game and came around to open the door. Honestly, I don't think I could have done that on my own—figured out how to pull the handle of the sedan's passenger door. He helped me stand.

One second I was hugging Classic Car guy, the next I was flat out kissing him. It was good, that kiss. So good that I thought for one hot second about inviting him in.

Fortunately, 'drinky girl' had a moment of clarity. I wanted to see him again. And if I wanted to see him again, then the one thing I couldn't do was invite him in. So I separated myself from him and told him good night. I watched him pull out then went up the stairs to my back door.

Sadly, 'drinky girl' became just plain drunk girl, and I lost my shit. I may have sat on my back steps giggling like a hyena. Why? Because I soon discovered that I could not open my door. I have one of those door locks with a code. Usually I type in the code, open the door, and I'm home. This night I discovered that didn't work. That after several failed attempts the door locks you out for a few minutes. I think it took me a solid ten to get inside.

By the time I had gotten my pajamas on and had curled up on the couch, this text was waiting for me.

Classic Car: Had a great time.
Me (still too drunk for texting, but there was no one to take away my damned iPhone)**:** I did as well. Even though I probably had a drink too many. I'd love to see you again. Please have a safe drive home in your everyday car.
Classic Car: No way, you're good. Let loose.
Me: I never do it. Uber got me.
Classic Car: Good for you. So that's why you kissed me.

Me (spiraling downhill quickly)**:** No, I wanted to kiss you the moment you sat down. But I have restraint (in person, clearly not behind the glowing blue screen of my phone).

Classic Car: Don't you do that ever again! Lol.

Me: I only touched your hair once. See? I'm good.

Classic Car: You're good regardless.

Me: Thanks. Had a great time really. I was nervous, and I'm not usually nervous.

Classic Car: I was nervous also. Didn't notice you were.

Me: I'm usually way more chill. But I needed that wine before you got there to chill me out.

Classic Car: Didn't notice.

Me: Yeah. Yeah.

Classic Car: Well then me showing up late was a good thing.

Me: It was. I had time to calm the hell down.

Classic Car: LOL. You're too funny.

Me: Not really. Too old to be nervous. But good looking guy plus date after a whole day alone talking to myself equals nerves. But now I'm good and should obviously not be on this phone spilling my guts.

Classic Car: Thank you for the compliment.

Me: You are very welcome. I had a great time really.

Classic Car: Next time when I see you, please don't feel the need to restrain yourself. I actually like that personal touch. Just kiss me next time.

Me: I try not to be too forward.

Classic Car: Don't worry about it. I actually appreciate that...if you have to hide how you feel, then you're not being you. Does that make sense? So let's get it out

in the open. I'm very, very attracted to you. To be
honest, I wanted your kissable lips on mine.
Me: Same here.

Great texting, right? I'm mean drunk texting, but good
nonetheless. I was psyched. It was the single best date I'd had
so far.

Then you know what happened? Classic Car guy packed his
bags and got on a jet plane for Guatemala. Yep from great date
to international travel. After this he texted for a week, pictures
of Central America, sweet nothings in English and—be still my
beating heart—in Spanish. Because he figured out quite
quickly that I grew up speaking it at home.

The next question was, of course, whether date two would
live up to the first.

NINE

The Zen Guy plus Thunderbolt Redux

FEBRUARY 9.

ALL THE WAY over from West Hollywood to Venice in the Uber I kept reading and re-reading the messages Classic Car guy had sent me the night before.

"So let's get it out in the open. I'm very, very attracted to you. To be honest I wanted your kissable lips on mine the whole night..." he'd texted after he'd gotten home. And like every time I'd read it before, a small shiver went through me with those words.

The whole night had ended early because I'd liked him. The more I liked them, the less I knew I could give them. Because despite huge leaps in humanity and feminism, men still like the chase. So this was why I was in this Uber riding down Venice Boulevard toward the beach to meet another date, who I call Zen Guy.

I'd swiped right and matched on Tinder. Our online messages on the app had been fun and flirty. We'd talked about traveling and our top ten destination bucket list. So I was excited to meet him in person. Plus, he was cute of course. Short hair. But I was willing to make exceptions from time to time.

It was 7:45 in the evening. I'd directed the driver to Nineteenth Street and the boardwalk like he'd texted. But when I got out of the car, it was dark and deserted, and when the Uber driver gave me raised eyebrows that questioned the sanity of leaving me there, I nodded reluctantly. It was Los Angeles, not Mars. I could walk a block or two and get another Uber if push came to shove.

I thanked the driver, slammed the car door, and watched the Nissan slip away into the dark night. I took in my surroundings, because that's what smart girls do. I'd seen too many episodes of *Law and Order: Special Victims Unit*, to be anything other than observant.

Nearly everything was closed and Zen Guy was nowhere to be found. Except for Thunderbolt who was precisely on the dot, not a single guy had shown up on time. But I'd already ridden some thirteen miles in LA traffic, and wasn't eager to make the return trip right away, so I decided to wait.

"What are you wearing?" I texted. Recognizing faces from online apps, no matter how cute, wasn't my specialty. Especially as what a guy thought was his best picture often wasn't his most current. Zen Guy was the world's slowest texter, and he didn't have an iPhone, so I had to wait for the green message bubble to appear. There were no dots to tell me he was typing. I hoped I didn't get an unattractive dowager's hump the way I was permanently hunched over my phone waiting for texts from guys these days.

"I'm dressed like a Brooklyn hipster and carrying an orange backpack," popped up in green. That response straightened my spine in an instant. Was he serious or was his tongue firmly planted in his cheek?

Brooklyn?
Hipster?
Orange?
Backpack?

I shivered in the cold ocean air suddenly regretting this impulse to go on fifty first dates. I'd had a good one on Friday. Why was I jinxing it with this Saturday nonsense? But I was already one thirty-dollar Uber ride and a half an hour drive in, so I waited. Took a picture for Instagram, then waited some more.

In a few more minutes, he walked up to me. Every other date I'd been on had been at a place, Tart. Andante. Harlowe. My apartment. This walking up was, well, odd. But hey, I was the cool girl, right? I could go with the flow.

"Jolie?"

It was him. I was kind of disappointed. He was cute. But he didn't live up to his pictures somehow. I can't say exactly why. He was in some way just less animated than his photo, if that's even possible.

I nodded my greeting. This wasn't a huggable moment. He was in a fleece lined green camouflage hoodie with the afore-mentioned hunting orange backpack. I kind of had to wonder if this was his usual dating outfit because I kind of felt like he wasn't even trying. Classic Car guy had at least been trying.

I'd made an effort. My sweater was black cashmere, and I had flannel lined leather motorcycle boots over leggings. We were not a match made in fashion heaven. At least Classic Car guy had worn a sport coat and snakeskin cowboy boots. I'd thought he'd overdressed, but now I was touched that at least he'd made an effort.

"You look amazing in person," Zen Guy said.

This was starting to be a theme. I wondered if there was something I could do about my online pictures that repre-sented me better. But I shrugged the thought away. Pleasant surprise had to be way better than grave disappointment.

"Thanks. What would you like to eat?" I asked.

Next to us was a beachside sushi stand on one part of the

strand and a funnel cake stand on the other. I'd skipped lunch for this, so I hoped fried dough wasn't the only thing on offer.

"This was stupid," he said. "I don't know why I suggested we meet at Muscle Beach when everything was closed."

I'd wondered the same thing, but just nodded my head, putting on my easygoing cool girl mask.

"No problem. Let's walk toward the light over there." Quickly we passed a few open restaurants, but he didn't so much as glance at any of the sidewalk menu stands.

"What do you eat?" I asked. I always swiped left on admitted vegans, vegetarians, and picky eaters. But it was entirely possible that his cute online photo had made me over-look that detail in his profile. It wasn't that I didn't like vegans' lifestyle. I was a live and let live kind of girl. It was that they were hell to take to restaurants even in southern California, where accommodating the fad diet of the moment was a thing.

"I'm an omnivore," he said. I tried to hide my relief, though it was short lived as he continued. "But I only eat organic food. No GMOs or Roundup can enter my body," he finished. "I used to grow and harvest all my own food."

"Hmmm." I nodded. That was all well and good, but we weren't bringing anything from his farm to a table in Venice anytime in the next few minutes and my stomach was protesting the delay.

"I do like fish though. It's why I like to hang out by the beach."

I didn't mention that fishing off the Los Angeles coast was *verboten* because years of pollution made it unhealthy. There were signs everywhere warning amateur fisherman not to take anything home to eat.

"Hey!" I pointed. "What about that sushi place over there?"

"I don't eat much at sushi restaurants." Because sushi

restaurants serve...fish. I didn't go down that rabbit hole. Instead, I took the lead, walked the few steps to the establishment, and asked the hostess for a table. Whether he followed was up to him. He didn't protest.

"I can probably find something to eat," he said as we weaved through the busy tables.

Once we were seated, I gave him my most interested smile, leaned in, and asked, "So what do you do?"

It wasn't the most genuine I'd ever been, but we had at least a couple of hours together, and I wanted to make the best of it.

"I travel the world instructing people on spiritual traditions," he said. "I'm famous in many circles for my knowledge of indigenous peoples of the earth. But I can't really talk about it. A lot of what I do is top secret."

This was not the first 'top secret' answer I'd gotten. I'd had to unmatch from a very cute guy on OKCupid who claimed to work for the CIA because I thought his definition of CIA may be 'married.'

I once had a cousin-in-law who did work for the CIA. I know there's a building in Virginia full of CIA employees, not to mention the countless spooks we all assumed were operating underground throughout the world. And I have no idea how they dated, because not being able to talk about a third of your life seems like it would be awkward, but I wasn't buying anything top secret from Zen Guy.

Spiritual traditions didn't seem like the kind of job to come with a confidentiality oath. I decided to give the topic of how he supported himself a wide berth. He was free to keep his secrets. I changed the subject.

"And you're living in Redondo Beach?" It was the reason we'd met in Venice. I thought it was a fair halfway meeting point. Redondo Beach was in the South Bay a good forty-five minute drive from West Hollywood. I didn't want to be that far away should a date go south or even if it went well. It was a long and lonely ride home at eleven at night and especially so at two a.m.

"Only temporarily," he said. "At a crash pad with a couple of roommates. One of the guys is in a wheelchair, and I'm helping him out a bit. I don't really have one place I call home although I have to go to New York City next month for a dentist appointment."

I didn't mention that that was the biggest non-sequitur, nor that there were thousands of dentists in Los Angeles. I'm thinking he knew that. And crash pad? Whatever chance he'd had of getting laid went up in smoke like the steam coming from the rice warmer behind the sushi chefs.

I didn't do crash pads and roommates. I'm not against either in theory. But I'm developing a few rules as I go about this dating thing.

First, I haven't been back to a guy's house. I'm not one of those people who's worried about a serial killer at every turn, but I feel like there are one hundred ways, or maybe just a handful of ways, a visit to some unknown man's house could go sideways. Add in more people I don't know, and I couldn't find a way any of that crash pad stuff would make me feel comfortable.

The second reason he wasn't getting laid? He didn't pass the Tiffany Haddish test. On an episode of Jada Pinkett Smith's *Red Table Talk,* Haddish had spoken about her weird hobby of taking pictures of penises or keeping notes on them or something involving the cataloging of cocks she'd known. That part, though a bit bizarre, wasn't what had really stood out for me.

It had been her assertion that if a guy didn't keep his fingernails clean, he didn't not keep his penis clean. I didn't have enough personal experience to confirm her theory, but it had sounded so plausible and well thought out that I'd kept it at the forefront of my mind.

When Zen guy picked up his menu, his fingernails were not clean. That combined with him completely not bringing his best self to this date crossed him off the list of people I'd ever possibly sleep with.

Fortunately, the waitress appeared then so I didn't have to get any more specific on the crash pad. Bubbly and effervescent, our server asked for our drink orders. I got an Arnold Palmer—half unsweetened ice tea—half lemonade. After hitting three strong drinks the night before I needed to keep my wits about me and remain as sober as a judge.

Zen Guy. You know the one who said he only ate organic, GMO free food raised by his own hands? He said, "I'll have a Coke."

I didn't give him a speech on the genetically modified high fructose corn syrup that was in his drink. I couldn't see how an argument would do either of us any good. This guy's stories were as full of holes as Swiss cheese. I'd have ordered popcorn if I could, because I could see that this was going to be an entertaining night if nothing else.

For the next three hours, we talked about growing up on the east coast and travel to places in the world far and wide. Despite all the things that would keep me from sleeping with him that night or any other night—ever, I still enjoyed getting to know new people.

As long as I stayed away from the third rail of sacred traditions and the joy of crashing on someone's floor well past thirty, he was okay to talk to. I did the thing I always did when I wasn't interested; I asked my dates about themselves. Men love to talk about themselves. It keeps the focus away from me and the chase they love so much.

To complete this act, I lean in making sure my face is at a great angle and keep my hand under my chin. If I widen my eyes and blink a lot, they never think to ask a thing about me.

I will have to say that I was surprised when he offered to pay for dinner when we were done. I honestly didn't think a guy like him would have cash, much less a credit card. I offered a ten dollar tip for the waitress and considered it my good deed for the day.

When we got outside, I pulled my thick cardigan around me. We were in the depths of the Los Angeles winter with a brisk fifty degree breeze coming off the nearby ocean.

"You smoke the ganga?" he asked.

I shook my head, but lifted my hand toward him. "Feel free to indulge," I said.

Zen Guy continued to surprise me. I have to say I didn't see that coming, though I should have. It seems that guys in LA have exactly two go-to icebreakers: booze and pot.

He took a toke or three, filling the air with the fragrant smell of marijuana smoke before he offered it to me. "There's tobacco in there as well," he said.

Bonus! A smoker, I thought. This just got better and better. I kind of wanted to Google the latest articles on how American tobacco companies had genetically modified plants to have twice the nicotine and therefore twice the addictive quality and text the results to him. Between that and the soda, I wanted to tell him, he was polluting that body he claimed to hold so dear. But I demurred; maybe he'd get an earful from his New York dentist.

"So, I'm going to go," I said pulling my phone from my purse. In seconds I'd pulled up the rideshare app and was summoning a car.

"It was great meeting you," he said. I gave him a swift hug. He went in for a kiss. I wondered if it was the mouths of

Tinder dates that had me fighting back this cold I couldn't quite shake.

"You are really cute," he shouted through the door as he closed me in to the blue Nissan Versa that would take me home.

As the driver made a U-turn away from the ocean and toward my place in West Hollywood, I settled in for the thirty-minute ride trying not to feel too sorry for myself. Friday's date had still been amazing even if I'd turned into drinky girl. Saturday had been a total bust.

I fingered my phone again, bringing up Classic Car guy's texts.

"I was nervous," he'd typed after he'd texted me about having a great time.

It reassured me that maybe there was a chance that I'd meet a great guy who was as into me as I was into him when I was ready. When I could be a girl who could express her feelings on the spot and not hours later behind the screen of the phone and the protection of the little blue bubbles. While the driver was cruising his way up Fairfax Avenue, my phone buzzed.

It was Zen Guy sending a blowing kiss emoji accompanied by the words 'nice meeting you.' My phone vibrated against my thigh again. The next text from Zen Guy was a bathroom selfie of him, shirt lifted at one shoulder an almost perfect mimic of six of the top ten selling romance novel covers. And there was nothing wrong with the physical merchandise. He was ripped. Sometime between top secret spiritual missions, and despite the two Cokes he'd had, he had time to work out.

"Trade you a pic for a pic," read the caption. I didn't delete it, because a girl can always use a little man candy. But there was no way in heck I was going to respond to that request for nudes. I'd seen that ploy one time too many. I was old enough to know better. Once I sent out a picture of my tits, I'd never be able to control where that snapshot went.

I ignored that and vowed once again not to stare at the last of Classic Car guy's texts for the thousandth time. I turned the phone over in my lap and it buzzed again. This time from a New York City mobile area code. It took my phone a second, but the number was quickly replaced by my date from two weeks ago, Thunderbolt.

"Did you get the massage at the place on La Cienega?"

I looked out the car window at the glowing lights of the windows at the Park La Brea complex as I tried to remember the last conversation I'd had with him. Then I remembered that he'd liked to indulge in massages of all kinds across the southland, both the legal kind and the not so legal happy ending kind. Then I smiled big because the universe had just dropped something great into my lap. My do-over with Thunderbolt.

"Oh God," I finally responded. "Not yet. I cashed in a gift card last week for some place on La Brea." That part was true. He'd changed my life in just the littlest way, reminding me that I could enjoy a small indulgence like a massage during work hours. It has been good.

"But she's the best," he said, vouching for his preferred massage therapist at a place on La Cienega in West Hollywood.

"Have you been getting your regular?" I asked him. He had seemed like a guy who didn't have any qualms about indulging in a little bit of everything.

"Nah, working too much," he said. "Need one, though."

I flipped through what I remembered of our time together. Most of my memory hadn't been about the conversation. And God knew, after a date with Zen Guy, which had exhausted my indulgent spirit, I wasn't in the mood to offer my untrained hands at massage.

"It's on my list," I demurred. "I'm in an Uber right now on my way home. Are you feeling good about your progress?" I asked about the film project he was working on.

That I did remember. We'd talked quite a bit about it as we'd gotten to know each other the little bit necessary to feel comfortable hooking up.

"Yeah, actually. Screened it tonight, and I'm like oh, just a bunch of tiny things. Like the structure is good. Just a bit more finesse."

"I know this feeling...but I have a friend who says that the perfect is the enemy of good enough. She says this when I refuse to let go of a book," I mused.

Well that much was true. Letting a book out of my hands was the hardest part about being an author. Knowing that no matter how long you worked on it, it wouldn't be perfect drove me bananas.

"I'd say come over, but I caught a cold," he texted next.

"I'm sorry to hear that you're sick." And God knew I was sorry. My fantasies of a rematch were quickly being squelched. I knew without Thunderbolt to distract me, I'd be back in the dark looking at Classic Car guy's texts...again. Lord knew that kind of obsessing wasn't healthy for any female out of puberty.

"Yeah, bummer. It happens. Especially when working 24/7," materialized from the three little dots on my phone.

"I agree. But I over think projects..." I said, returning to the work conversation. I loved creative people, sick or well, hookup or not.

"Well you seem very heady in general," he said echoing the first time he'd been over and I'd been too in my head to enjoy the sex as much as I'd have liked. "Get loose, baby," he texted next.

"I'm totally working on it. Seriously." And I was very seriously thinking about it. I did not want a repeat performance of Friday. Me indulging in too many drinks and still not able to tell a guy that I found him attractive. That I liked him much more in person than I had even over days of texting.

It hearkened back to the insecure seventeen-year-old I'd been, and the insecure twenty-five-year-old who'd signed up for more than a dozen years of an emotionally and physically abusive relationship. I wanted to be anything but that girl again.

"Nice," Thunderbolt typed jolting me back to the present and my vow to loosen up.

"It's a very current goal..." I said, Friday's night drinky girl scene at the forefront of my mind.

"All good. I'd bone you anyway but glad to hear."

"I'm totally up for that," I said because suddenly I was very much up for that. A good hour or two of indulging in pleasure and thinking about all the ways I'd effed up my life from the day I'd married my ex years ago through last night at the bar around the corner.

"Alas, you're too sick, no?" I asked, knowing I was baiting him. Knowing that his baser instincts would very much override his common decency to not spread germs throughout the city. "Says the girl at Fairfax and Third," I typed after I looked up to see just how close I was to my place and his. That first night we'd discovered we lived less than a mile apart.

"I mean I'd like to fuck you but I don't want to get you sick..." But it was as if the winking dots were showing his weakness.

"As I'm getting over a cold, I'm not sure I care," I said. And I didn't. I was so over the virus that I'd been trying to shake for nearly two weeks. Even if we somehow recontaminated each other, it would be worth it.

Like I knew he would, Thunderbolt relented. "Ok wanna come over and get fucked?"

"I'm totally up for it. Where?" As I waited for a response, I wondered why it was so easy to be honest with him now and why it has been so hard for me to be as honest the night before.

His address popped up on the smartphone screen. I looked out the windows again and we were nearly at my house.

"Let me ask about diversion," I said looking at my driver for the first time in the half hour we'd been in the car together. He pulled over and looked back at me. It was past eleven at night. I imagined that James, the name on the Uber screen glowing back at me above a picture of a blue Nissan, had done this dance at least a few times before. "Can I change the destination? I read the address and the driver typed it into his own smartphone.

"He's changing it now," I typed to Thunderbolt. "We just drove by my building." I said letting him know my ETA was less than five minutes.

"I'll come down when you're here," he said.

And in five minutes, there he was. My super cute, sweet-faced hookup from a couple of weeks ago. Even though he typed a mean game, throwing around the words 'bone' and 'fuck,' he couldn't help the nice Boston Irish boy his mother had raised.

He held the door for me. He offered me the bathroom, water, a seat on his couch, even cold medicine. Sometime between me getting there and getting comfortable, the lights had gone all soft and he'd lit candles.

The things I'd remembered about him did not disappoint. He was a generous lover, but still whispered his desires. With a cold blocking my ears, it was even more difficult to hear his time around. But somehow, we worked it out.

After the first round—because I did remember that about him—that he liked to do it twice, we talked about story structure and the creative process. He asked me about my dates, and I ended up spilling how stupid I'd been the night before.

"So did you bone the guy you like?" he asked from his pillow.

I pulled the other pillow under my own head and looked back at him. "God, no. I want to see him again."

"And that's why you're here with me."

"And that's why I'm here with you," I confirmed.

"Then let's go again," he said.

TEN

The Aussie

FEBRUARY 16-17.

MY HOUSEKEEPER COMES on Saturday mornings. Having someone in my small apartment all day running a vacuum and water is a bit more invasive than having someone in the three story house I shared with my ex. But after a few months, she and I had a routine of sorts.

I'd go spinning at the gym on Sunset, come home and shower in the bathroom yet to be cleaned. And by the time I was ready to get dressed, my bedroom would be cleaned and the bed made. For the remaining hours, I'd hole up there writing and working on book stuff.

In the last week, Classic Car guy had texted me every single day. Pictures of Spanish colonial buildings. Snaps of him and his older brother. Videos of the Caribbean after he and his brother had driven across Guatemala from the Pacific Ocean side of the country.

Then there were the texts.

On his first or second day away, I got this after we'd gone back and forth a bit about travel.

Classic Car: FYI. I do miss you...Want to see you, spend time with you when I come back.

Later there were more travel selfies and texts.

Classic Car: I'm very glad that you like me, that I'm your type.

I'll admit to saying as much in one of these long rambling text conversations.

Classic Car: I'm definitely attracted to you. Your intelligence is very sexy, and it's a turn on. Not to mention physically I'm also very much attracted to you.

After that, we probably dissected that first date a few times and chatted about our days. His was sightseeing and hanging with his young niece. Me texting pictures of a book signing and various spots I'd hit in Los Angeles while he was away.

I share all this to say that while I was looking forward to seeing Classic Car when he landed in Los Angeles in a week, I was also looking to have some fun.

Enter The Aussie.

Of all the apps, I think I hate Bumble the most. Supposedly, it's a more relationship oriented app. But the guys on there...flaky as all get out. Despite matching with dozens of guys and messaging a few, not a single one of them ever wanted to meet in public.

'Want to continue this lovely and wide ranging conversation over coffee/a drink/dinner,' I'd messaged to more than a few.

Not one of them ever said yes. I hadn't put my finger on what in the hell that was about, but there I was on Saturday listening to the incessant sound of a vacuum while swiping through Bumble's yellow interface.

A cute guy caught my eye, and I stopped to read the bio. It said something along the lines of Aussie in West Hollywood for the weekend looking for fun. I also remember something about him saying he didn't want sex. That was a disappointment, but what's a girl to do?

Fun is fun.

Me: Still in town? I love to meet new people.
The Aussie: Still here! How does one know if they are a good kisser?

That 'swipe left if you don't like kissing' like in my online dating bio got fair bit of screen time.

Me: In answer to your question...people will tell you... What are you doing in town?
The Aussie: But then people don't tell you if you're not! I've been told...(blushing emoji face). I was originally going to visit Seattle, but the weather screwed those plans up so I thought I'd spend a few days in LA. What have you got planned for your weekend?

I paused a moment from texting and got some water. I was thinking that Seattle's loss due to record breaking snowfall the week before was about to be my gain.

Me: I'm going to a play this afternoon then just hanging out. (I didn't add that I'd love a distraction from hoping for, waiting for, reading, or rereading Classic Car guy's texts). I added the thing about kissing to my profile because a shocking number of people don't like kissing (which is fine), but I don't want to hang with them...

The Aussie: Seriously...guys say that? That's disturbing...who doesn't like a good pash (as we call it in Australia)?

Me: Some guys are weird or very truthful. Honesty is appreciated. I'm about to head out for a couple of hours. If you're up for getting a drink later, let me know. I'm in (WeHo) West Hollywood as well.

The Aussie: Sure why not? I'm planning to be at the Rainbow later...I'm not sure if you like that place or not, but it's like my home away from home. If you want to join me that would be great.

Me: Time. I'm not familiar with the Rainbow.

The Aussie: Really? It's like a famous rock bar on Sunset. I might head there around 6.

Sometimes I feel like I have two brains and two lives. One inside my marriage and one outside. One of my ex husband's issues was that he didn't like me to go out—not without him.

And him?

He didn't like to go out. He was worried about being killed by a drunk driver. Not being there for the pets twenty-four seven. Eating food that wasn't cooked at home. And so on and so on. The minute leaving the house came up, his anxiety would take over.

When we first moved to Los Angeles, I was interested in making friends and going out. I met up with people I'd known from college who were in the area. I made new friends from our neighborhood. From the gym. From volunteer activities. My ex somehow managed to suck all the fun from each and every activity.

He didn't like my friends. They were too rich, too poor, too educated, not educated enough, trying to cheat him when we split the bill, too elitist, too clueless. I could go on, but I'll spare you. I'm sure that you get the picture.

He often said that he hated everyone. I used to think that couldn't be true, but now I'm pretty sure it was. I got exhausted managing him through lunches and dinners and parties, so I'd stopped going out with him.

The times I went out without him were hard as well. I'd go out with friends and he'd text me every few minutes.

When was I going to start the drive home?

When was I going to be home?

What was for dinner the moment I arrived home?

Was I having a good time with my friends?

On the nights I went out for dinner. I got the same texts and no matter how late I stayed out, he refused to go to sleep until I came back. The moment I went upstairs the questions started. All of this...this is why I didn't remember the Rainbow. I think I'd been there with friends when I'd first come to the city, but I'd given up on going out to places like it over the last half dozen years.

I finished the play. *Linda Vista*, by the way, was the best play I'd seen in three years. Following Thunderbolt's advice, I'd started relying on the aid of Uber drivers. I could drink. Not drink and drive. Keep it safe and not have to look for parking.

So I parked my car at home again, made sure I still had it pulled together, and ordered an Uber. Two minutes later, a white Lexus pulls up.

"Hi...again," David said. It took me a good minute of scrolling through my phone to realize David and I had met before. It was David from last week's one AM pick up at Thunderbolt's house.

Forget bartenders. Now I think Uber drivers had the real front seat view to human dating rituals. I buried my face in my phone's messaging app—a sure way to avoid the awkward conversation of my active dating life.

Me: On my way. What are you wearing?
The Aussie: Gray top. Jeans. I'm here at the far end of the bar. See you soon.

Even though at first blush, The Aussie wasn't my type. (He was built like a linebacker), we hit it off almost immediately. We were born only three weeks apart. We'd both separated at exactly the same time. We'd had the same issues in our marriage. I

n a conversation that would be an over share in most contexts just worked with him. There was a lot about our lives that was similar even though he was an accountant and I was a writer.

After talking for a couple of hours, he suggested we move to a table on the inside for dinner. And for the first time since I started these dates, the waitress grabbed my phone and offered to take photos of us. We friended each other on Facebook, and I sent over the pictures.

While we were looking for each other on Facebook—which was surprisingly hard as Facebook assumed two people on different continents with no mutual friends couldn't be looking for the other—The Aussie revealed his hobby.

"You should look me up by my record label."

I leaned in and took a closer look at the accountant I'd spent the last few hours laughing with.

"You have a record label?"

"Yeah, just promoting a few musicians my business partner and I like. We put them on vinyl."

I sat back appreciating my date who had just become multi dimensional.

"You know what? You should lead with that."

We'd ended up staying out well into the morning, just before last call. We talked about everything. It was too bad he lived eight thousand miles away and not eight, because he'd have made an excellent regular date.

The Aussie: I had a really great night...you definitely didn't bore me. Sorry if I talked too much. If you feel up to it tomorrow that might be fun. Talk in the morning.

We did it again the second night. I took him to dim sum on Beverly. We talked for even more hours. I even told him about Classic Car guy. His advice. Take it slow. He also had some words of caution about trying out a relationship with someone who was so different.

If The Aussie and I were in the same town, I'm sure we'd go out again. He was the kind of guy who'd grow on you slowly. I could see that. He'd be kind and chivalrous and wouldn't take a woman for granted. Maybe I'd meet someone like that. In the meantime, I wanted to pursue the chemistry Classic Car guy and I had.

ELEVEN

The Gay Bar

FEBRUARY 23.

I SWEAR to God I nearly died from two weeks of texting. The anticipation of seeing Classic Car guy was almost too much to bear. So on Friday I get a text from him.

Classic Car: What's the plan?
Me: Do you want to come over around 6:30 or 7?
Movie? Dinner in?
Classic Car: Yes. That sounds fine.

He'd mentioned that it was getting chilly outside and a movie night would be a good idea.

The code was clear. He was interested in more intimacy than the first date. And despite what I'd said to Thunderbolt, I was willing to make an exception because...sex with a cute guy.

I lazily sat around all day waiting for the hours to pass. At seven, I started to get nervous, at eight I was feeling like I wouldn't see him. Then at 8:22, a text came in. I was loath to read it, but I did because I believe in ripping off Band-Aids.

Classic Car: Hey can I have a rain check for tomorrow, if possible? Just got out of the shower. I'm a bit too tired to get behind the wheel again.

He'd been behind the wheel driving all over Southern California—as far away as Palm Springs—sourcing classic car parts.

I don't know who I was angrier at—him for the no show or myself for wanting to see him so much. There was so much I wanted to say. But I decided to do 'cool girl.' She did not react. She moved on.

Me: Sure. Let's talk later.

So I pulled off all the clothes. The velvet leggings, the carefully fluffed cashmere top. I traded it all for pajamas and tried not to feel too sorry for myself.

Then I did the thing all the advice columns said when a guy ghosted you.

Get back to your life.

For me that involved going to the gym and tiring myself out during spinning class.

Writing.

Then meeting up with a friend for a very long walk along Venice Beach.

It was during this walk that my phone pinged, of course. My friend said that I shouldn't answer him. But I couldn't resist.

Classic Car: Hola.
I texted him a picture of the Pacific Ocean and pier in response.
Classic Car: Donde estas?
Me: Venice. You?
Classic Car: I'm so jealous. Nice.

To throw a little more shade on the situation, I texted a full bod picture my friend had just taken of me. I didn't add any more words.

Classic Car: Very nice. I'm here at home. Cleaning up.

I put the phone away so I could focus on my friend again. We walked another hour or so and chatted before I started the drive back home. While I was driving, the car buzzed and read a text to me.

Classic Car: Hi there.

I channeled all the cool girl energy I could find in the air along Venice Boulevard.

Me: What's up?
Classic Car: How was your day at the beach?
Me: The beach was great. I spent some time with a friend just walking along the shore. I'm on Venice Boulevard now driving home.

I turned up the music waiting for the next text that I knew was coming.

Classic Car: Any plans?
Me: Not yet.

I sent the text then paused a long moment through a few stoplights. Then I prompted my car to text again.

Me: You could change that.
Classic Car: Perfect. Let me do that. Your place. Same as yesterday.

Me: Sure. Why not?

Classic Car: Call me when you get home. I'll let you drive. You look great in your picture, by the way.

So I did it again.

Exfoliated.

Washed the hair.

Brushed it out.

Plucked the stray hairs.

Spritzed on the perfume.

Pulled on the sweater and the leggings.

Zipped up the boots.

Got ready.

Forfeited the tickets I'd bought to a talk on love, sex, and relationships. I had to make a trade off between doing it and talking about it.

I cracked open a bottle of wine and waited patiently. Well, I was impatient, but traffic in Los Angeles is no joke and I couldn't make him materialize any faster if I wished upon a star.

I tried a lot of things to calm my nerves. It had been two long weeks of texting, and I had zero idea if the fantasies that had filled my head would live up to the reality.

I took out two glasses and poured one. I left it on the counter so I didn't down it like that first date. I took myself to my dining room banquette and attempted to write. When I stopped checking the parking in the back, I finally did settle in and wrote a good few pages. Then he pulled in. I let him up through the back door and mud room, and he came into the kitchen.

"Hi," I said. It was the best I could do. It was all I could do. The nerves had come back with a vengeance.

"You okay?" he asked.

"I...it takes me a few minutes to switch from writing to real life," I said. That wasn't entirely true, but it was the best I could come up with. Because standing in my kitchen sipping wine was the guy from the amazing date. He looked and smelled as good as he had before. Only he was in my kitchen. In *my* kitchen.

We talked about something. His brother. His travels. Audi lovers. That's all I can remember because I was too nervous to take in much. Eventually I pulled some kind of Trader Joe's puff pastry appetizers from the oven and fed him. At some point, he took the wine and our glasses to the living room so we could get comfortable.

After a couple of hours, and a bottle of wine later, he popped up.

"Let's go out."

"Out?"

"Music. People. Let's get an Uber."

Fortunately, weeks ago I'd cribbed a list of popular bars and hangouts from a friend with a husband in the business. I picked a place and ordered up the car. When the two-minute warning came up on my phone screen, we bounded down the stairs and along the walkway toward the street.

"You haven't kissed me yet," he prompted.

So I did. Made me all warm and fuzzy on the inside. Warmer and fuzzier than all of the wine.

The Uber pulled up, and he grabbed my hand and helped me into the car, but didn't let go. Ten minutes later, we hopped out on Santa Monica Boulevard in West Hollywood.

During the day, the restaurants on the street are full of people waiting for eggs and pancakes, avocado toast and Benedict. The same restaurants at night, turns out, are a different story entirely. It took a few seconds before my eyes adjusted. The bartenders were indeed without shirts. The tables had nearly naked male go-go dancers on them.

Classic Car guy looked at me and shrugged. "Where do you want to sit?"

There was a booth in one corner, but it was under the speakers, so we pulled up two barstools instead. He got a beer of some sort, and I ordered a large club soda. The problem with splitting a bottle of wine is that it's hard to tell how much I drank. And no way did I want to go back to that first night. I needed to keep my wits about me somehow.

Wits, it turned out, may have been overrated. Classic Car guy took a seat on the barstool facing me. I took another seat facing him. He leaned forward, tucked my hair behind my ear, slipped his hand along my neck, drew me close, and kissed me deep.

Bartenders must have a front row seat to human mating rituals because that's what this bare chested one witnessed. Classic Car guy and me kissing desperately on the edge between making out and going too damned far. Two drinks in —I gave in and had a couple of vodka Collinses—and a couple of hours of talking and kissing, we decided it was time to go back to my place.

The Uber ride back was even shorter than the one there, a mere five minutes. In seconds, we walked hand in hand from the car, up the stairs and into my apartment. I'd dimmed the lights long before he'd arrived. There were only two Edison bulbs lighting the living room. He shrugged out of the sport coat he wore, lay back on my couch, and took me with him. Weeks of pent-up anticipation overtook us both, and before I knew it we were both naked from the waist down.

I both had and hadn't bargained for things to go this far. In either case, not this quickly, though.

"I have to tell you, something," I said laying a hand against his naked chest.

His breathing was fast.

"What?"

"I have my period." Trust me on this. It wasn't something I really wanted to share. But he had moved to the top of the need to know list.

"Is that why you shied away from me?"

I didn't think I had. Maybe when he'd been rubbing the inside of my thigh at the bar. I couldn't exactly remember with my brain flooded with wine and vodka and lust. There weren't any more words. Instead, he moved, I moved, and in the next few minutes we were joined together moving in rhythm.

Despite the fears Thunderbolt had introduced, we were good together that time and the five other times that night. In between and after, I slept better than I had in months. It was actually a text from a friend that woke me.

> **Friend:** Want to have lunch with you. What days are you free?
> **Me:** Tuesday, Wednesday, and
> Friday. Text tone woke me. Guy is still here. I'm exhausted. I don't know how people do this...
> **Friend:** Want him to go home? You could pretend this text is an emergency.

I was sitting on a wing back chair in the corner of my bedroom. I looked at the blue linen duvet cover where he was hidden underneath. I most certainly wasn't ready for him to go home...

> **Me:** Not yet...
> **Friend:** Sorry for waking you! You're usually an early riser.
> **Me:** No worries. I usually don't stay up late. All these guys love to hang out way too late...why can't I have sex at a reasonable hour like say 8 pm and not midnight?

Then I texted her a picture of my bed, the only parts of Classic Car guy that were visible were the four fingers of his right hand.

Me: He's in there somewhere...
Friend: LOL.

We agreed to meet up for the Notortious RBG exhibit at the Skirball. I tossed the phone onto my rug then climbed back in bed with Classic Car guy and woke him, kissed him, and initiated a rematch. After, he asked to use my shower. Cleaned himself up, then he kissed me or I kissed him and in an hour he needed another shower.

At some point, I saw him out. Then I promptly returned to the now defiled couch and went straight to sleep. It was another text tone that woke me up.

Classic Car: I miss being inside you.
Me: It was great having you inside me.
Classic Car: I think the weekends are for me being inside you...sleeping next to you.

First thing Monday morning he texted again. All the feelings I had about being stood up on Friday had nearly evaporated.

Classic Car: Good Morning.
Me: Good Morning to you. How was your Sunday?
Classic Car: Not very good. You left me craving you.
Me: That's a good problem to have.
Classic Car: Not when you're not around. I can still smell you. How was yours?
Me: (deciding to tell the truth for once) I hung out with a friend and thought about you.

Classic Car (in Spanish)**:** Let me say again that I love your body with so many curves. *Mi Boricua.*
Me: Siri does not read Spanish. (I'd been driving from the gym).
Classic Car: But you do. Keep going to the gym, I notice the new curves in your thighs and legs. You, my dear, are extremely intelligent, and I find you very attractive. I had a big smile on my face when I woke up next to you in bed.
Me: Your face and hands and...were good to wake up to.
Classic Car Guy: And...? Say what you feel.

I put my phone down and did a turn around the kitchen. This was not a case of me not saying what I feel. It was a case of me not talking about penises. But I did. Because when it comes to texts, it's clear that I don't have any boundaries.

Me: And...OMG I spend my whole day writing about penises and I have about 1000 words for them. I enjoyed waking up to yours...but honestly, I try to keep my texts R rated at most. So there it is...
Classic Car: You spent the day writing about us? Not asking for X rated, but thanks. Feels good to hear that. The small of your back drives me crazy...Also love your shoulders.

Now I have to take a break from all this texting to say that when I talk to him, this guy acts like he has no game. Honestly, he has all the game...

Me: I spend the day writing about couples dating and relationships. It's the bread and butter of the romance genre. The couples change. The settings change. But at its core, it's all about relationships and sex. I don't write about myself or people I know. That would be some kind of violation, I think. It's all imagination. Also, talking about feelings isn't my strong suit.

That last was the biggest understatement of all time. Which was why, I imagined, so much of our relationship was taking place via text. Was maybe surviving those in between times because of texting. Other guys had quickly given up on me when I got all emotionally constipated.

Classic Car: I understand. Was just curious. It wouldn't bother me at all to be honest. I guess if it was good things, right. (then in Spanish) Well, I hope you enjoy your work day and I hope to see you again soon. Take care. I already miss you.

A few hours later, my car alerted me to a text. Siri read it in her creepily officious voice.

Classic Car: Just wanted to say hello. Had a nap and was dreaming of you.
Me: Now that's something I'd like to hear more about. Glad you got some sleep.
Classic Car: It was very nice actually. It's like a clip that keeps rolling in my head.

This wasn't the first time he'd texted about dreaming about me. He'd dreamed about me while he was in Central America. In them, I was in a bathing suit swimming next to him in the Caribbean. I didn't have such vivid dreams myself, but it did sound nice.

There was only a single blemish on the Saturday night with Classic Car guy. I'd made a huge mistake, a teenage girl's mistake, a rookie mistake. I'd had sex with him without a condom. Not once, not twice, but six times. I had zero idea why I'd done this. I'd never done it before in my entire life.

My son was conceived in less times than I had sex with Classic Car guy. Every other time I'd had sex in my life, I'd worn a condom. I'd offered one to Drummer Boy, one to Justin Time, and two to Thunderbolt.

I wanted to blame my period and too many drinks, but I didn't think that was it. I think I stupidly somehow thought it would bring me closer to him. That's all I can figure.

Either way I promptly called my primary physician on Tuesday and made an appointment for STD testing because I hadn't lost *all* my marbles.

TWELVE

The Omakase

THE TEXTS CONTINUED like that for a few days with the best selfies from him in between.

His mad selfie game hadn't suffered. I kept them in a folder on my phone for when I needed a little pick me up in my day. We'd confined our first couple of dates to the weekend. But there was something about Classic Car guy that distinguished him from everyone else I'd seen, except Thunderbolt maybe.

When he got close to me or merely breathed in my direction, I got crazy turned on. Despite the fact that we probably had nothing in common except our mutual attraction, it was some kind of pheromone catnip.

But by Thursday, I couldn't wait for the weekend. As soon as I got home from lunch with a friend and a few errands, I picked up my phone and opened the messaging app.

Me: So here goes with me being...well...bold.
Classic Car: Shoot.
Me: What would make me happiest right at this exact moment is making a plan to see you again.

Classic Car: Absolutely. Good company is never turned away.

Me: So what are you doing for dinner tonight?

Classic Car: Tonight, I do not have plans. Let me ask you a question. Are you alone as of tonight? Or tomorrow?

Me: I am very much alone tonight and tomorrow.

Classic Car: Oh, I didn't know that... Would you like me over tonight?

Me: That's a big yes.

Classic Car: Ok. What's your morning schedule like?

Me: Nada. I've got nothing until Saturday.

Classic Car: Well I can't wait to see you. I miss those kissable lips. I'm craving food...

Me: I'd be happy to take you to dinner.

Classic Car: Whatever you like is fine with me. You decide.

We'd had a discussion, by text of course, of his favorite foods. The top on the list had been Italian. But his mother was Italian, which told me not to mess with that one. He also liked a bunch of other things, any of which I figured I could find within a two mile radius. Living in Southern California had some great benefits.

Me: You tell me when you'll get here, and I'll figure out food.

Classic Car: One thing about me? I can always eat. Love eating.

Me: Do you love it as much as sleep?

Classic Car: Almost. There's a three hundred-pound fat man inside me. He loves to eat.

Me: If you come, I'll take you to sushi.

Classic Car: You said the magic words. Love sushi. Seafood is life. Hey, we should plan to get away to Mexico. Quick trip down there. Go to Puerto Nuevo. Lobster time!!!

About the invite. This was not the first time Classic Car guy had made a not so offhand invitation for us to get away for the weekend. It was one of the things I rarely responded to. I didn't quite know what to say. Three solid days in a resort with him would either be heavenly or hellishly too soon. I could never quite decide. Today, I hovered over the text bubble and left a heart. That was the most I was willing to do on that one.

Me: Let me see what I can work out for tonight.
Classic Car: Okay what time do you want me at your place?
Me: The sooner the better. Seriously...whatever. It's Thursday and I think Sugarfish last seats at nine.
Classic Car: I can be there about seven-ish.

When he got there, all the anxiety I'd wrapped myself in over parsing every damned text message went away.

Sugarfish was a creation of legendary sushi chef Kazunori Nozawa. I'll skip the long backstory, but Nozawa was one of the first sushi bars in Los Angeles to strictly enforce the omakase tradition. The chefs made you what they thought was best, and you ate it without question. I think the original location in Studio City closed a few years back, but I used to love going there. If Classic Car guy loved sushi, I thought this would be the best place to take him. Casual rolls with sweet ponzu sauce and spicy mayonnaise was something we could share later.

The minute he met me at the door, he pulled me in for a

hug and kiss. I locked up and we held hands from my door down the path to the sidewalk to wait for the Uber. We got to the restaurant, put our names on the list, and cuddled outside under the warmth of the propane heater.

Even though I was well past my teenage years, that feeling that whooshed through me when being with him was the same as it had been the first time I'd been in love at seventeen. Not that I was in love, mind you. Just seriously in like.

The sushi was amazing, of course. But the conversation was pretty interesting. It was the first time he seemed vulnerable. It was the first time that he mentioned having a stutter. He'd said it had been pretty bad when he was a kid growing up, and as an adult—in sales mind you— it still came up from time to time. I hadn't heard it yet despite the hours that we'd talked. After dinner, while we waited for the check, he moved from sitting across from me to the vacated bench seat next to me and looped an arm around my shoulders. He seemed to like physical affection. It wasn't my strong suit, but I made a mental note to keep that in mind.

Paying the check. Getting an Uber back. Walking up to my apartment. That part was all a blur. He was like me, after only a four-day hiatus, as horny as all get out. As soon as I closed and locked my front door, we were all over each other.

It was a Friday morning, and Classic Car guy was standing in my bedroom getting dressed after a shower. He'd come over Thursday night and we'd gone out for sushi. It had been an interesting night.

It was our third date and I'd learned a few things about him. He'd been pretty vulnerable telling me a few things about himself, like he'd grown up with a stutter that still came out at times. He'd also dropped a bit of a bombshell in the morning when I'd casually asked what he was most ashamed of. I don't even know why I'd asked the question because I certainly didn't have an answer if he'd asked me. But he'd laid there in my bed, quiet for a long moment.

"You haven't killed someone, right?" I asked. Because for some reason that felt like a deal breaker.

"I was with a friend," he started. "Ended up spending ten months in jail."

Honestly, I started to think I'd have been more surprised if he'd said he'd killed someone.

"How old were you?"

"Nineteen. I was with a friend. Did something stupid. Got caught up."

From what I pieced together, he'd been drinking for two days, decided to drive because his more-drunk friend couldn't, they got into a single car accident, and his friend was hurt—bad. I even suspect after thinking about it that his friend may have died in this accident or because of it. I knew his friend was dead, but he'd hinted that this wasn't what had killed him. From what I know about the law, though, it didn't make sense any other way.

"What did your parents think?" I asked. Because I couldn't imagine being on either end of that conversation. Telling my parents I'd been arrested and was facing jail, nor having my own son tell me—his mom—the same.

"I told them that I'd handle it. That it wasn't really their problem," he said.

My mind skittered all over the place. Immediately I felt insensitive, though. Because just last week I'd gone on about how few romances were gritty and real. How I'd recently finished this book about a hero who'd just left jail, lived in East LA, and was trying to stay out of gang life.

"I hope I didn't offend you when I talked about that book," I said, wondering how elitist I'd come off. Class was already an unspoken issue between us, and I feared I'd widened that gulf with my offhand comments about a guy who could have been him, ex-con, east LA, all that.

"No. I didn't take offense," he said.

"God, I used to spend a lot of time visiting prisons," I said as my brain worked to take in the new information. "Where were you?"

"San Diego," he said. I had visited quite a few prisons in my old job, but hadn't been to San Diego. I couldn't even remember what state prison was down there.

"Did your parents visit you?"

"Yeah." He nodded. "But I didn't want them to see me that way." It was a refrain I'd heard before and didn't understand. Statistics showed that recidivism rates were lowest when felons stayed connected to family and community. But that preachy thought did not leave my mouth.

Instead, I was quiet because he was saying something about paying lawyers and how he'd been originally dealing with eighteen months and how it had been reduced to ten. And all I could think about was what my first real job had been.

Criminal defense attorney.

I will tell all dates that I'm a college graduate because it's true. What I don't often reveal is that I went to graduate school, or if I do mention graduate school, I don't mention that it was law school. I'm already getting the vibe that I'm too much—too pretty, too smart, to talkative, too outgoing—and I wanted to go out and have fun, not discuss my resume.

There was silence as I sat across from him, cross-legged trying to think of what I could say that wouldn't be weird. There wasn't a long list that came to me.

"I'm totally not judging you," I said. "Remind me one day to tell you about the job that I had visiting prisons."

Then I offered him a spare toothbrush, and he went to shower.

He'd said he was an open book.

I was a closed one.

So after hours of talking, he dressed and I watched him, thinking about whether I should go on a date with Naughty Dred. I hugged and kissed him good-bye then took to my couch.

THIRTEEN

The Naughty Dred

I SAT on my couch dozing for a good couple of hours while I talked myself into the date. I liked Classic Car guy, a lot. I hadn't liked anyone in that way in so many years that the feeling was both unfamiliar and so very familiar at the same time.

Reluctantly, I showered, dressed, brushed my hair, and put on perfume. I clicked on the many bracelets that often felt like cool girl armor and walked from my back door to my car.

Even with the music at full blast, I couldn't stop thinking about Classic Car guy. For some reason, I couldn't quite pinpoint why thinking about this guy who I liked made me incredibly sad.

If you'd been driving on Santa Monica Boulevard in Beverly Hills at precisely that time, I'd have been the girl in the SUV alternately singing at the top of my lungs and crying. I think I was sad because nothing had gone right for me relationship-wise in life and the hope that this one could work out for whatever period of time it would felt daunting or unrealistic.

Either way I heeded the advice of the stack of dating books my friend had sent my way unsolicited. They all said until you have some kind of commitment with one guy, you should very much see others. So I got to the bar where Naughty Dred suggested we meet in West L.A. and went about the task of finding parking.

I walked around the corner and down the block between my car and the bar and took in a deep breath. I shrugged off the feelings about Classic Car guy and settled into my cool girl skin. Fluffed my hair and pulled open the heavy wooden bar door. I looked down at my phone and scrolled for his Tinder message.

"All the way in the back past the bar by the fireplace," it said.

Once my eyes adjusted, I followed the directions and into the back room. It was bar dark, obliterating any of what was left of the late afternoon daylight that was outside. It was a smallish room with six couches and the requisite California faux fireplace. The kind that flicks on with a switch and kind of looks real until you stare at it for more than a few seconds. And it never puts out much heat.

If I'm being honest, while I swiped right on Naughty Dred in January, I probably wouldn't swipe right now. He was a white guy over forty with dreds, solidifying the story about how he'd pushed aside corporate America to do his own thing.

The reasons I'd swiped on him were that he was Canadian by birth, which I figured probably meant he was nice, polite, said 'sorry' and 'thank you,' said 'about' with an accent, and he indicated in his profile that he believed in a woman's pleasure.

All this had been laid out quite poetically in his profile interwoven with a picture of his two young Weimaraners. Two months later, I was already feeling quite jaded and wouldn't have swiped because while he wasn't homely, he wasn't cute either. And attractive to me was my current standard.

The best part of being the cool girl and not having anything invested in a date is that I didn't care about the outcome. I had no nerves and could really zero in on him, give him the cool girl experience. It felt like a superpower.

I greeted Naughty Dred with a hug. It felt like a standard California greeting. He was wearing a striped hoodie and jeans, canvas sneakers and white sport socks. White socks. Wasn't my taste, but hey, I wasn't that interested in dating him. And with his house in complete disarray, there was no pressure for sex. With that off the table, I could settle back and have a good time.

"I checked to see when we first connected," Naughty Dred said. "It was on January eleventh. I like odd numbers so that seems auspicious. Especially as today is March first."

Numerology wasn't my thing, but he seemed to think somehow the date we connected on Tinder was auspicious. It had been nearly six weeks between that initial message and our meeting because Naughty Dred was...a serious adult.

He'd just sold one house and bought another. The current one was in the midst of a renovation. He had family and friends and a life. After ending a relationship where my ex-husband had few interests outside of me, it was refreshing to meet people with full lives of their own.

He'd actually invited me to dinner before. But it had been after a date with 99 Books, and I wasn't in the best mood that day. It was raining and I'd spend an hour and thirty-seven minutes carrying a conversation with a guy with zero confidence in himself and life. I didn't have the energy to do it again.

Naughty Dred used to be a senior vice president at a studio in Burbank. He told a few stories of what it was like working at the top of the Hollywood food chain. Then we talked about renovations and money pits. Los Angeles is famous for them. I had a 1920s Spanish one. Now he had a mid-century on in Topanga.

The thing was that the conversation was easy. It wasn't

awkward. It wasn't uncomfortable. I was more forthright and honest than I was able to be with Classic Car guy. Five hours. That's how much time we spent together. Five hours. It was fun. I actually laughed out loud several times. I didn't even realize I'd skipped dinner until I got in my car at nine on Friday night. I didn't even let all the comments about how hot I was bother me too much. I tried to take them in. Say thank you. Internalize that feeling of being admired, desired.

The perverseness of the date drove me batshit crazy. Part of me thinks it was easy to be open to Naughty Dred because I didn't care. Or maybe it was because he was older. But it made me feel like there was something very wrong with the way I was going about the whole dating thing. Because I wasn't sure what I wanted. I knew I didn't want marriage. After trying it though, I wasn't sure I wanted casual either.

When I woke up, there was a message waiting for me from Naughty Dred.

"I enjoyed meeting you, communing with you, and witnessing your beauty."

They were nice words.

Sweet words.

I guess I just wished they'd come from someone else.

FOURTEEN

The Music Editor

MARCH 3.

Me: Norah @2
Music Editor: I'll be there.

CLASSIC CAR GUY was occupying too much of my brain. Especially since every interaction with him felt like me pulling and him pushing. I'd fallen in like with someone who said all the right things. Spending time with him, though, was hard.

I felt like I was always making myself available and he was doling out his affections a drip at a time. When he was here, he was laser focused on me only. When he wasn't, I felt like a child jumping up and down and waving to get his attention. Nothing about that felt good or healthy.

So, like every good single girl, I was swiping away whenever I had a spare moment. I'd probably matched with this guy a week ago. But between changing phones, (The bigger the iPhone storage, the longer it was taking to swap over content), and texting Classic Car guy about how I'd like to see him again if he were game to no response, I hadn't prepared for this date.

All that said, I was in an Uber on my way to a self-described 'eclectic American restaurant in the heart of West

Hollywood.' I frantically went between one phone and the other trying to get a signal. Finally, about three minutes into the five-minute drive, I found the guy I was meeting on the app. I looked more closely at his picture to make sure that I would recognize him, then quickly scanned down his description. He was five feet eleven, red hair. I checked the pictures again trying to remember what had attracted me. The fourth or fifth photo was of course a guitar. Right. Musician. A person who makes the magic. But the other part of his self-description, I'd overlooked. He wasn't jacked or fit or had 'a little extra' build, he was overweight. I was wondering what in the hell that meant when the Uber driver announced we'd arrived.

The downside to meeting guys in my own neighborhood was that I hardly had a moment to think between leaving the house and getting to the spot. I was on the fence as to whether having more time to think was good or being tossed in unprepared was better.

Either way, on this one I was unprepared. I'd never in my life dated anyone who was heavy. And my guess was that Music Editor probably came in at over three hundred pounds easy. I gave him a classic LA hug and suggested we sit at the bar.

He was very much in the same stage of life as me. Recently broken up. Ex-spouse he shouldn't have married in the first place. Happy with his career. He had bright red hair and a super engaging personality, but he wasn't my type. The conversation, though, was fabulous.

Music Editor also introduced me to my first avocado toast. I'd always thought this California menu oddity—though now I see it everywhere around the world—wasn't something I'd actually pay for. But he ordered it and offered me a taste. It was kind of a cool idea, though I still couldn't see myself ordering it.

We sat at the bar post brunch until they started setting up for dinner. I tried my hardest to focus on him and not what I wished I was doing with Classic Car guy who hadn't responded to my offer to spend Sunday together while he chased down cars.

I have to say that his job was quite fascinating. You know that music that increases the tension in a drama or lets you know something funny or scary is about to happen. It was his job to work alongside the director, pick the music, and make sure it played at just the right moment. I looked him up on IMDb and he's worked for years on some of the most popular music and TV shows. Additionally, he had his own band who performed music he wrote. It was totally cool.

The combination of great looking and great conversation wasn't easy to come by, I was thinking.

FIFTEEN

The Divorce Tour

MARCH 9.

I SHOULD HAVE CALLED it the divorce tour. It was like every week I had to sit down and talk with someone I hadn't spent time with since I'd left my ex. I decided to drive up to Santa Barbara to see some lovely friends who I'd known for nearly a dozen years.

We'd had the luck of turning up pregnant at the same time. Though they'd moved from Pasadena up the coast, the wife of the couple and I had gone through our pregnancies together and the early baby years. We'd both gone from daily runners pre-kids to waddlers while pregnant.

They were a joy to know and since leaving Los Angeles had moved to a beautiful coastal area. I'd been up before but only with my ex. This time I decided to go up alone. I made the drive along the Pacific and arrived early in the afternoon. I hung out with my friends and their kids, then took in a great Mexican dinner and a lovely scratch margarita.

While I was driving up the coast, Apple Car Play let me know that I'd gotten a text from Classic Car guy.

Classic Car: Hola. Buenos dias.
Me: Can you call me, I am driving.

I snapped a picture of the coast.

Classic Car: I love that drive...

Then we talked for a good half hour. He was all sweet words and he asked a lot of questions about when I'd be back on Saturday.

"No later than one o'clock," I said.

"Good. We have to hang out," he said.

Classic Car: Hope you're well. Miss your cute butt.
Me: Made it. Been hanging with my friends.
Classic Car: Have fun. Catch a really nice buzzzzz.
Me: (Texted him a picture of my margarita). I am very well...thanks. A margarita or two is a good thing.
Classic Car: How's the night?

I never answered that text because I was answering those really hard questions friends ask about divorce. I was trying to walk that very fine line between letting them know that I was okay with my decision and not discussing the abuse.

I still found it mortifying to talk about and avoided it at every turn. We stayed up way late talking. Then we went to a beautiful restaurant in the mountains the next morning.

Wanting to see Classic Car guy as much as he'd professed the day before, I made sure I was home by one. I showered, relaxed, shopped, then as time wore on, I texted him around five.

Me: Home relaxing after a pretty good drive back. You?

It was three hours before he responded. I tried not to be upset. I knew the likelihood that I was going to see him was dwindling with every minute that passed.

Classic Car: Hi good morning.
Me: Evening??
Classic Car: Same difference.
Me: So...
Classic Car: Hola. How was the drive?
Me: Short. No traffic on the way back.
Classic Car: Nice.
Me: Pretty along the coast.
Classic Car: I bet.
Me: Will I see you tonight?

I was tired of talking about driving. No one was interested in anyone else's drive up the 101. I couldn't figure out why he talked such a big game, but was so terrible at follow through.

Classic Car: Hi getting something to eat, haven't had much appetite. Unless you want to get in bed and sleep, I still feel little tired and sleepy.
Me: I'd love to. Should I drive to you??
Classic Car: I feel like soup. Is there a Mexican place by you?
Me: Of course.

Two hours later, we were creeping up on ten o'clock, and I wondered what happened to him in the meantime.

Me: Close?
Classic Car: Yes. I haven't forgotten about you. Already passing through downtown.

Me: Gotcha.
Classic Car: Have some wine.
GPS says 15 min.
Me: Ok.

It was 10:30 when he arrived. For a woman who's used to getting up at the crack of dawn with an elementary aged kid, who had gotten up with her friends' elementary aged kids, this was late. But I tried my hardest to rally.

"Mexican soup places are closed."

"Really?"

I wondered if he was really from Los Angeles. L.A. had a lot of things, by not so many late night restaurants. It was a perpetual complaint of us East Coasters. There were three things you could get after ten, ramen, Jewish deli food from Canter's, and soon du bu, a Korean tofu soup. Canter's was closer, tofu soup was arguably better. So we rolled up to the twenty-four hour chain. It was hopping at eleven.

I ordered him a seafood tofu soup. I had a mixed one. He enjoyed the heck out of it. For a long second while sitting there when he was talking, I wondered how in the heck the two of us were in this place together. We were from two completely different universes. I was all upper middle class education and work from home mommy. He worked in mobile phone sales, though I'd learned that he'd taken a year off to do...I'm not sure what.

But I enjoyed myself nonetheless. We went back to my apartment, watched a terrible Netflix movie, then went to bed. The sex was pleasurable if not exactly satisfying. After the second go round, I had to slip a hand between my legs and relieve the pressure that had built.

Then we woke up, did it again, and talked. It was Daylight Savings, so we'd slept later than usual. Or it was because he'd come so late. Either way it was a lazy Sunday where neither of us much wanted to get out of bed.

"Is your mom crazy?"

I didn't have a felony conviction, but crazy mom was something I could relate to.

"Yep." By crazy, I knew what he meant. I couldn't say how I knew, but I did. What we meant was a narcissistic personality disorder.

"Do you talk to her?"

"No, not for the last six months."

"Eighteen months for me. She sided with my ex in the divorce."

"Same here. I told her I was leaving him, and she told me I was crazy. Then proceeded to console him to the tune of an hour a day for days at a time."

"My sister and I tried taking our mom to therapy."

I knew how that went without him telling me. One of the books I'd read that had helped me immensely was *Will I Ever Be Good Enough? Healing the Daughters of Narcissistic Mothers*. I can't say the book healed me. It helped me understand a lot of why I'd grown up the way I had and why I'd walked headfirst into an abusive marriage. How it had gone with his mom was predictable. She'd stormed out within the first few minutes.

"Did you go yourself?"

He nodded.

I was shocked and hoped it hadn't shown on my face.

"I did," he answered. "For six months. But I left because I could see people using it like a crutch. I didn't want to be there for years."

"I'm in therapy now. It's helping," I admitted.

We talked for another four hours about lots of things. He proclaimed himself to be an open book who would answer anything. I asked a lot, though I think in retrospect the questions were superficial. Eventually he showered, kissed me, then left.

Classic Car: Arrived home about 35 minutes ago....Hope I didn't keep you. I felt comfortable with you in bed while we talked....Sorry if I overstayed.
Me: You have never overstayed. I loved having you here and talking.
Classic Car (sends me the song I Love You by the Climax Blues Band): Great song.

I didn't have time to take to my couch. Instead, I had to get right in the shower to get ready.

The hard part was that I had a date in a couple of hours. I'd had to cancel with Day Trader, again because I was well out of time, but I'd kept my second one with the Music Editor.

March 10.

Me: I could do Sunday.
Music Editor: Fantastic. Supposed to rain. Want to do dinner?
Me: Yes.
Music Editor: There's a great Ethiopian place near you. Does that sound good?
Me: Sure, which one?
Music Editor: Merkato. Have you been?
Me: I don't think so. What time?
Music Editor: It's a hole in the wall, not fancy but it's very good. I'm open, whatever works best for you.
Me: I'm open.
Music Editor: Ok, great. Shall I pick you up?
Me: Sure.

At the appointed hour, me having washed off the smell of sex with Classic Car guy, Music Editor arrived.

Music Editor: Your Subaru awaits…

It was funny. I got in and we drove the mile or two to Los Angeles' Little Ethiopia.

We talked about a movie his friend was producing and other projects going on in entertainment. Unfortunately, the conversation wasn't as good as last time. There was more about our exes. Interesting. Therapeutic. But not sexy.

"I think on dates, people should talk about where it's going," he started.

I dodged that. It wasn't going anywhere, but I didn't want to ruin the end of my dinner and my tall glass of wine with that conversation. After we ate, we did some spice shopping, then he took me home.

If he'd been more attractive, maybe I'd have made more of an effort. But that isn't exactly where we'd gone wrong, I think. We'd gone wrong by going down the 'what went wrong with our marriage' road. It was one that was filled with potholes and we'd hit them all.

When Music Editor went to the bathroom, while waiting for him, our food came so I took a picture and texted Classic Car guy who'd mentioned that he'd never had Ethiopian.

Me: So the food is better than it looks. It's eaten with your hands. I'll take you sometime.
Classic Car: It looks great.
Me: It was. Better with a hearty Ethiopian wine as well. I'm about to turn in. I listened to the song. May have to download.
Classic Car: Ethiopian wine? Sounds interesting. Have a good night's rest. Had a great time. Thanks for

the extra attention this morning. I was talking way too much...

Me: The wine is like a cross between a crisp white and mead. You were not talking too much. I enjoyed it greatly. Good night as well. I'll be sleeping on the side where you were.

SIXTEEN

Mister Irish

MARCH 16.

OF COURSE, on the day before St. Patrick's Day, I decided to meet Mr. Irish. I'd swiped right on Tinder because he was from Northern Ireland. To hell with my criteria. I just wanted to hear the accent for a few hours. If dating isn't interesting, then why bother. For the record, he had short reddish blond hair, was okay looking, but not devastatingly cute, and worked at UCLA doing research of some kind or another. No long hair. No artistic bent. In fact, my last notification from Tinder was that he'd updated his pictures. I couldn't resist clicking. He'd added some...with his cat. On Tinder, he messaged first.

> **Mr. Irish:** You were the first person who popped up.
> You are so very cute.
> **Me:** Auspicious? Thanks for the compliment.

We talked a little about research and my feelings about protagonists in fiction. It was a lovely intellectual conversation. Interesting but I could have those kinds of conversations with my friends. I think I was looking for a different kind of conversation in a relationship. Then he referred to the 1980s Northern Ireland conflict as 'The Troubles' and I was back in.

We agreed to meet on Saturday. I preferred nighttime dates, but he wanted to meet in the midafternoon. I had no idea why but agreed to a date at The Village Idiot. It was a large bar/restaurant that I'd been to for a few private parties over the years.

I like to get to dates early. My plan is always to get a seat, scope out the bar, have a glass of wine to relax and be there first. With almost all my dates being late, that hadn't been a problem.

The 'cool girl' ordered a drink, then I took out my phone to send a text.

Me: I am here sipping a cosmo.
Mr. Irish: At the bar in front of me?
Me: Confused...

I *was* confused. Turned out he was an early arriver. He'd ordered a drink and was sitting in a corner table behind me. Awkwardly beat at my own game, I closed out my tab and joined him at the table.

Guess what!

He'd just moved out from his ex-wife. He'd just started therapy. He'd moved in with his cat or cats—there may have been more than one. Despite living in Los Angeles for at least a decade, he knew nothing about the city.

I was over 'the ex' conversation, so I changed the topic to one of my favorites: travel. Surprisingly, he hadn't done much of that either. He'd moved from Northern Ireland to the US for a woman. Had met another, moved to Arizona, and so on and so on. He didn't seem to have any particular dreams of ambitions of his own other than following love.

Fortunately, the bar started filling up at seven. That was my cue to close out our tab and see whether there was some kind of nighttime entertainment waiting for me. I can't remember what Classic Car guy was doing on this weekend, but he was, of course, unavailable. The closer he seemed to get, the more he pulled away.

While we were outside of the bar waiting for Ubers, Mr. Irish asked, "What are you going to do with your night?"

"I am going to decline to answer that question. I only hope it's fun." I was already trying to figure out who I could meet up with. I swiped, but other than a proposition for mutual masturbation over Bumble, nothing came up. I ended up writing, knitting, and turning in early. Turned out, I'd need that sleep in the bank.

SEVENTEEN

The Day Trader

MARCH 17.

I'M KIND OF SHOCKED that this date ever happened. Last weekend when Classic Car guy was debating on whether or not he was going to make the drive to my place, I turned to my perpetual backup plan, Tinder. I swiped a few times.

By now, it should be clear how it started. I swiped until I found what I was looking for: a guy who was cute, long hair, musician. Same shit, different day.

It was past eight o'clock, and I wasn't in the mood to beat around the bush. I didn't have it in me to text for hours or days before we met. I wanted a backup plan for the night.

Me: What are you doing on Tinder?
Day Trader: Looking for you.

Well, that was the right answer. I may have gotten off Tinder messaging for forty minutes while I negotiated with Classic Car guy on whether or not he was coming as it was getting close to nine o'clock.

Day Trader: What are you up to?

113

Me: Trying to keep my nights interesting...this one is looking touch and go.
Day Trader: What can we do to make it more interesting?
Me: Promise me that I don't have to have nine hours of chat before I can meet you in person...

Yeah, a total dick. My impatience with Classic Car guy and the endless texting of guys on dating apps was coming through, and my filter had gone offline at nine.

Day Trader: Not at all. We can meet up tonight. It takes you nine hours to respond though.
Me: Give me a minute...

To, you know, text Classic Car guy and make sure he was in his car and actually driving to my house.

Day Trader: K.
Me: Tonight just got complicated in the way I hoped it wouldn't. How's your Sunday Looking?
Day Trader: Everything ok? Got something to take care of, but should be done around 6 on Sunday.

Then fifty minutes pass as I...you guessed it...text Classic Car guy about meeting up.

Long story short. I was a dick when the guy I really wanted showed. The moment Classic Car guy walked in the door and we walked out to get an Uber to a twenty-four seven soup place, I turned off my phone and focused solely on him. That last Sunday had been Daylight Savings Time. That, combined with eating Korean tofu soup at midnight, watching a horror movie till two or three, then spending the rest of the night fucking until five set me on a trajectory to not be able to see Day Trader on Sunday.

There was a '?' from Day Trader, which I ignored because of course Classic Car guy woke up and we really talked for most of the day. When he was here, he was present. I can't underplay what it's like to be the sole focus of someone who never checks their phone. Who talks and listens as if we are the only two people on earth. But when he's not here, it's like he's smoke.

So when what I described to another friend my weekend with, "thus begins the normal shit show with Classic Car guy. Where it's push/pull," my friend was not a fan. She'd had a front row seat to his behavior a few weeks earlier where he disappeared for twenty-four hours, then started texting in earnest when she and I were walking on the beach together.

"He sounds high maintenance," she said. "Peter Pan. Fly away boy. He's probably sexy, though."

With that, she nailed it. It wasn't just that he was sexy. But it was a lot that. If he so much as breathed near me, I wanted to stop whatever I was doing and drop my panties. That part was crazy making. None of that mattered if we weren't in the same zip code, much less the same room.

Day Trader, as it turned out, was very much in the same zip code. When it became clear that this weekend no manner of coaxing was going to get Classic Car guy from his couch, or bed, or whatever to mine, I was back on Tinder. I debated a long moment before texting Day Trader again. He would have been well within his rights to give me a huge middle finger.

Me: Got sucked into too much drama. What's up with you tonight?
Day Trader: Just out with a friend. About to wrap up. You?

So, look. I was a dick again. Or just a tired person. I promptly fell asleep on that conversation. I do that a lot, honestly, fall asleep on in and out of app texting. I find the back and forth mind numbing. Plus I like to get to bed early so I can turn up to the first classes at the gym.

On Sunday, I took one last run at it anyway. Because persistence pays, right?

Me: I went to sleep. Now I'm going to make a quick run to the store before I come home. You?
Day Trader: Just got home. No plans for tonight?
Me: Totally free and clear.
Day Trader: Do you feel like doing something tonight?
Me: I do.
Day Trader: Ok, I'm going to hop in the shower. It says you are a mile away from me. Not sure if that's accurate. I'm in West Hollywood.

He gave me his cross streets. Which were almost my cross streets. Then he gave me his number so we could get off the app. That was a good sign. To this day, I still don't have Naughty Dred's actual number. I thought of offering him mine, but in the end didn't do it. So when he wants to chat with me, to Tinder he goes.

Day Trader is better than I because he texted right away. I gave him my address. Then the dots. The three dots were winking at me for a long time.

Day Trader: Seriously? I grew up on that street.
Me: Really?

Day Trader gives me his childhood address. I flick open my

curtains and look across the street. There it is, his childhood home.

Me: I'm guessing you won't need directions.

I give him my apartment number.

Day Trader: Damn. My childhood best friend lived in that apartment.
Me: Now this is weird.
Day Trader: Weird in a good way?

I paused a long time. This was the first time I was inviting a man over who'd already been in my bedroom. The house he'd bought as an adult was only around the corner. One minute he was texting, the next he was knocking on the door. After Thunderbolt, who lived around a different corner, I was starting to think maybe I should date farther outside of my neighborhood.

I'd like to think I improved on my at home lounge outfit, but probably not by much. For some reason I think I was wearing the same Old Navy or Gap shirt I'd worn when Thunderbolt came over. My next goal will be to look for better loungewear.

Anyway, Day Trader. He was both more and less cute than his picture. But I was quickly getting used to this. People put the oddest photos on dating apps, none of which really looked like them. My less than six month old photos were starting to seem like the most honest thing anyone had done in the online dating world in a long time. This was the first person I'd been on a date with who wore cologne. I thought, wow, showered, dressed in clothes that are clearly ironed and cologne.

Let me say at the outset that I expected this date to be similar to that with Thunderbolt. Wine or no wine. Get naked.

Have sex. He goes home. I go to sleep and add another notch to my bedpost. It went nothing like this.

Instead, he was the perfect gentlemen. His mom would have been proud. His grandmother even more so. I know this because he spent St. Patrick's Day with his mother and grandmother. He was that kind of guy. One who cared for his family. One who was honorable. One who wasn't going to desecrate my couch on the first date.

The thing is, I kind of liked him. So much that we stayed up the entirety of Sunday night—talking. For him, I disregarded Monday. He was very much an honest, forthright guy. He owned a duplex he shared with his grandmother. He'd just closed one business and started another. He worked part time as a day trader. He'd once been a music editor, but didn't do that for a living any more.

He was nice.

Niceness always sucked me in. The other thing that got me, he didn't spend endless time complimenting me. It was great not to have to hear how I was better looking in person, great looking, sexy, etcetera. I like a compliment as much as anyone else, but sometimes it can get to be too much.

Instead, he came over, clearly having put effort into it. He was showered, well dressed in clothes that may have meet an iron, and doused in cologne. Despite that and the fact that he wouldn't take the invitation to sleep with me, I really enjoyed talking to him—all eight hours that we talked. I learned that while we agreed on some of the best television shows ever made, he'd never seen The Wire. It seemed inconceivable. So when I showed him the door at five in the morning, we agreed to a second date: a screening of *The Wire*.

EIGHTEEN

No First Dates

WEEKEND OF MARCH 24.

I DIDN'T HAVE the time or energy for first dates this weekend. I'd made plans a few weeks before to see a play with Classic Car guy. I was looking forward to it because I hadn't seen him for two weeks. He'd elevated push/pull to varsity levels. The previous weekend I hadn't seen him at all. He'd said that some personal issues with his ex had put him in a frame of mind that didn't make him good company. But he paired that with all sorts of sexy texting about the times we had been together in bed. From the previous weekend...

Classic Car: I think we need more lovemaking.
Me: And more exercise.
Classic Car: Keep the exercise. I'll keep the lovemaking.
Me: Promises...promises.
Classic Car: Smarty pants. I don't think I ever promise and not deliver.

Wow. So I didn't take that bait. I think I could write a

whole series of blog posts on my opinions on that...My response last weekend had been more democratic.

Me: Alrighty then.
Classic Car: We woke up feisty today.
Me: Very true. I'm always extra feisty.
Classic Car: What a nice day today.
Me: It's beautiful outside.(thinking face emoji) There's no more cleaning to do at my place...and you got me all hot and bothered with your flirty texting...
Classic Car: You're lucky I'm not there, I was thinking the same, I'd love to be inside you at this very moment...
Me: But how do I get that...

Needless to say, I didn't get that. He went on to buy a grill or make soup or something that didn't involve me.

It was that frustration that had led to last week's dates.

This week, he was back in it. I'd sent a text confirming that we were going to get together, and he replied of course, because we'd had a plan. He texted, then called first thing Friday morning with...a plan. He'd see a guy about repairing his first car, go to a doctor's appointment, then he'd head my way. His relationship with time remained loose, but not too bad.

He'd be at my house with his overnight bag if I did him a single favor—order him Salvadoran food.

I hadn't had Salvadoran food in years, and not near where I was living now in West Hollywood, but I was a resourceful writer who really wanted to see the guy she liked, so I figured it was a pretty fair trade off.

I got his pupusas, chicharrones, and fried plantains. He got to my house by five. Despite the two-week hiatus, he looked as good as I remembered. He hung up his garment bag in my closet then we sat down and ate. He was happy eating the food he'd grown up with, and I was happy to sit next to him and chat. Forty-five minutes later, he took himself to my bathroom and showered. Then he put on his own bathrobe then got all dressed up. He looked amazing and smelled even better. I drove us the few miles to the Geffen.

"You have a heavy foot," he said as we exited the parking lot.

"I do like to drive fast," I said. "There's a short cut if you don't mind walking through the Target alley."

"Making sure we don't run into your other boyfriends..." he quipped.

I let that one slide. I wasn't sure if he was fishing or joking, but either way I wasn't going to bite. He grabbed my hand, and I led the way.

He held my hand or my arm or leg while we watched a production that showcased the music of Nat King Cole. For a good two hours, there wasn't a moment that we weren't in skin-to-skin contact. We came back to my place and watched a little bit of comedy on Netflix. He did the thing he always did when he was with me, he was laser focused on me. No phones. No other distractions.

The sex the first time that night was amazing, all the more so because it had been two longs weeks since I'd seen him last, and Day Trader hadn't been up for a one night stand.

Ten or twenty minutes after, we were both breathing normally, I felt his erection against my backside.

"Can I sleep inside you?"

It was the single oddest request I'd ever had in bed. "You think that's going to work?"

I felt rather than saw him nod in the dim light.

It one hundred percent definitely didn't work. Not that time nor the time after that.

He was in a talkative mood the next morning.

"Have you been married before?"

"Before what? I've only been married once." I sat up and pulled the pillow to my chest. He'd asked a question not because he wanted an answer, but because he wanted to tell me something. I knew all about that tactic.

"I got married at twenty," he admitted. "In Vegas."

I'm nine hundred percent sure my eyebrows shot up to my hairline.

"By Elvis," he added.

"Of course by Elvis."

"In leather pants."

"Tight leather pants?"

He nodded. "And a matching leather jacket, and belt. Saleswoman got to me at the Gucci store."

"So, married at twenty?"

"My girlfriend and I dropped acid in the mountains. She said 'Let's get married.' I said 'Let's do it.'"

"In leather pants."

"They still fit. I'll wear them for you one day. They look good."

I was ninety-nine percent sure they did look amazing on him. He was hot in clothes and out of them. The conversation got more real then. He talked about his decision to cut off his mom. I told him that I saw a shrink once a week. In the tradition of trading information, he let me know what he'd been in therapy himself, for six months after leaving his ex-wife. I was frankly surprised. He seemed like the least likely person. But again, I was wrong about him. Which made me think a whole lot about the kinds of assumptions I made about people.

"So you were married twice?" I asked integrating the new knowledge.

"Three times actually," he said his tone sheepish.

"Wait? What?"

"I left my first wife, then married her again, then divorced her a second time. It only lasted a month that time."

"Wow. That was a hard lesson for you to learn," I said. I could imagine they must have had chemistry that was off the charts. I checked myself for feelings of jealousy. They weren't there. Being older had privileges. One of them wasn't unchecked jealousy at the thought of the guy I liked with another woman. This same discussion would have eaten me alive in my early twenties.

"I finally got it, though."

We talked about a bunch of other stuff like travel. He wanted to know when I could get away for a long weekend. We decided May would be good.

"Let's have breakfast," he announced at eleven.

"Breakfast. I think I should shower," I said. Because honestly, I smelled like sex and that didn't mix with breakfast.

"So point me to the kitchen. I'll get it ready while you shower."

"What? Breakfast?" I honestly thought he had been talking about going out. I figured I'd find and hit a local brunch spot. West Hollywood was full of them.

He put on his robe, and we walked to my kitchen.

"So you said you had tea every morning. I'll make that for you if you show me what to do."

I pointed to the kettle and the loose leaf tea. "Do you need..." I waved at the appliances.

"I got it."

So I let him at it. Went to shower, and when I came back, there was Classic Car guy in his bathrobe prowling around my kitchen.

"Your breakfast is ready. I hope I got the tea right."

He had. Breakfast was hot and delicious. The tea was perfect. I had to wrap my mind around the fact that this man who'd only known me two months had managed to make me tea that my husband had said was so complicated that he'd never managed it in all the years we'd been together.

He kissed me and whipped a napkin into my lap. It was good, eating with him at my kitchen's breakfast bar.

I once read in some book on dating that men have this moment. This moment where they make a decision about a woman. They go away, clear up whatever's in the way, then come back. It felt a lot like that kind of thing had happened. It felt like he was one hundred percent there all of a sudden. I wanted to believe in that commitment. That he wanted to be something akin to a boyfriend or whatever one called themselves past their mid-thirties.

That's what I held on to when he went silent on Sunday. He'd left behind his bathrobe and shampoo. I'll maybe admit to huffing his bathrobe like it was aerosol. I was going wash and fold it, but it smelled like him, so I was putting off the robe's date with the washing machine. I hadn't even told him he'd left it behind. There was so much I wanted to say, but was tired of the postmortem texting. So I decided to let it roll. Instead, I answered the texts from Mr. Irish and planned my second date with Day Trader.

Mr. Irish: You never write, you never call...lol. How are you, Jolie, did you pick your models?

I'd spent the last week having a photographer shoot cover models for my upcoming What Was...trilogy.

So I talked to him about the photo shoot and the show I'd been to at the Geffen Theater with Classic Car guy, editing him out of course.

Day Trader drove the half mile to my house and parked in my guest space. In all those hours we'd spent together last week, I must have mentioned that he could park there.

"You didn't walk?" I asked as I opened my door and waved him in.

"Didn't want to keep you waiting."

This guy was a freaking mystery to me.

We watched *The Wire* and just talked. He was great to talk to. He even went grocery shopping with me and then put away the groceries. In all that time, he never made a move. It was the oddest thing, but he was great company, so I decided that I did not need to rock the boat one single bit.

Thunderbolt has an impeccable sense of timing. Whenever I wonder where this whole dating thing is going, he pops up. Every single time I talk to him, I think it's going to be the last.

Thunderbolt: How's your sex life?

He's all about the opener. Surprised to hear from him, I thought about why he was asking because he'd taken an exit from mine. I started with my favorite tactic, deflection.

Me: I thought about you today. How is yours?
Thunderbolt: Steady stream of squirters.

I HAD to laugh out loud, then hoped that no one was reading texts over my shoulder. I wavered between telling him it was a great pun, great alliteration, or mentioning that the whole thing sounded messy. I didn't reply with any of those.

Me: Good to know you're not alone, then. I worried about you for a hot second.
Thunderbolt: You?
Me: I'm trying to decide how to answer that... I figure there's a way to fuck that up such that I never get to sleep with you again...

BECAUSE IF I'VE learned nothing about Thunderbolt is that he's not as gangsta as he wanted or pretended to be. I wasn't in the mood for his, I'm jealous but I'm not drama.

A few days after I'd left his apartment, he'd texted me about Classic Car. He was not a texter. It was completely out of character.

Thunderbolt: You have another date with that guy yet?

Me: Jesus. (That was my unfiltered shock at him asking about another guy). I'm actually texting with that guy now. He's out of the country for a week or two visiting family and beaches. So I'll see when he gets back.

Thunderbolt: Cool.

Me: I'm feeling better. Hoping you were too.

Thunderbolt: Hope he's a good lay. Best to try sooner than later.

Then he went radio silent when I mentioned a hookup. I assumed maybe he was jealous or being weird or something and left it at that. So his response several minutes later was a bit of a surprise.

Thunderbolt: Nah, I'm into it. Tell me some dirty stuff.

I'd made the mistake of taking him at his word before. I knew better than to believe he wanted details.

Me: It's not that interesting...weekly with the same guy I mentioned before. But not often enough, to be honest.

I thought I'd done a good dance there, answering without answering. But he called me on my bullshit with the next text.

Thunderbolt: How's the sex?
Me: Well...it's fine. But just kind of...fine.

The level of guilt I felt when typing those eight words was crushing. I liked Classic Car guy. Really, really liked him. But the sex could have been better. I was even thinking of spending some time trying to work on it, but I hadn't quite worked out how I was going to do that yet. Classic Car guy appeared, on the surface at least, to be full of machismo and ego.

I was starting to think, though, that I'd not quite gotten him right. That my perception of him was a projection from me. That sex that was amazingly intimate and caring could also have *zing*. But that took familiarity and time, and I was willing to give it that.

It didn't need to be like sex with Thunderbolt that was hot and satisfying right off the bat even without a shred of intimacy. None of that was to be shared with Thunderbolt, though. He drew a quick conclusion with his next text.

Thunderbolt: Boring.
Me: Yeah, but other redeeming traits. So I've been looking for someone to fill other days which is when I thought of you while driving today. But totally figured you were out.

That part was one hundred percent true. I was fifty percent sure that I wanted multiple sex partners at one time. I was fifty percent sure I was trying not to fall too hard for Classic Car guy by seeking out other guys. Thunderbolt fit into some exception category that didn't have me cheating because he'd come before. Or because Classic Car guy and I'd had zero discussion about exclusivity. I think he assumed. But again, I was having a hell of a time reading him, so maybe I was seeing what wasn't there.

Thunderbolt: Yeah, I could do for the occasional shag.
Me: There's too much driving and thinking in this city...That could totally work.
Thunderbolt: I don't see why not.
Me: Well then...my week is looking up...
Thunderbolt: Cool. Let's play it by ear.
Me: Totes.

NINETEEN

It's Not Cheating if There's No Commitment

MARCH 29.

THERE ARE many things to love about Classic Car guy. One of the things I don't love is how unavailable he is. I wanted a guy with his own life. The universe had provided just that. Maybe I'd asked for the wrong thing.

I couldn't figure out why that itch of being with someone wasn't scratched by my every-so-often dates with Classic Car guy. So I opened the phone and scrolled for male companionship for the weekend.

Mr. Irish would be available. He had a certain desperation that I knew would work in my favor. So I offered up a matinee date to see Captain Marvel, and he accepted.

He liked the concession stand and knew a lot of trivia about super hero movies that would serve me well in other conversations. I sucked at that sort of thing, but he was good at bringing me up to speed quickly.

Then I took the free drink at Dave and Busters. He had a beer. Me a mineral water. Given how my night was likely going, I needed to pace myself.

I caught up with a girlfriend I hadn't seen since we went to a Brené Brown Netflix taping together. Brown had talked about a call to courage. I think it was that courage that allowed me to pursue Classic Car guy. Looking back, I realize I'd met him just two days later.

Over brisket and pastrami at the newly opened Eleven City Diner on Wilshire Boulevard, my girlfriend talked about the guys, hers and mine. Day Trader, Classic Car guy, Thunderbolt, and the others who hadn't really made a reappearance.

My friend said that she liked Day Trader above all others. Because he was nice. Because he didn't expect anything. I told her that I liked Classic Car guy the best. We both agreed as I scrolled through the thirty or so selfies he'd sent, many at my request, that he was by far the sexiest.

"Then why are you texting Thunderbolt?" she asked me when my phone trilled during dinner. I was finding that I had to make my plans for the next thing while doing the current thing. It was rude, but with today's last minute planning, it couldn't be avoided.

"Because I like sex and need to make up for lost time," I said.

"Lost time?"

"There wasn't much sex in my marriage," I said. She's someone who'd met both me and my ex-husband at the same time. We'd lived in the same Los Angeles neighborhood when my ex and I had only been married a couple of years.

"Really?" she asked. I know she'd wondered about this. I'd hinted for years that my marriage was virtually sexless. Even though her own marriage had ended years before mine, sex, or lack thereof, wasn't the reason.

"He liked porn. He liked me jerking him off or blow jobs while looking at porn. He didn't much like sex with me." By that, I meant intercourse or anything that focused on my pleasure above his.

"I'm sorry. Really." She leaned forward, her face full of sympathy. I hated those faces from friends. Made me feel very sorry for myself and all the lost years. "That's such an asshole way of living."

"I thought it was what I deserved."

"What do you think you deserve now?"

"Maybe something better."

"And you like Classic Car guy?"

"I really do."

"Then maybe you should go home and watch a movie. Would he think you having sex with Thunderbolt was cheating?"

"Maybe. Probably. I don't know. But if he wanted exclusivity, he could very much use his words to ask for that." He occasionally referred to himself as my guy. But I couldn't make life decisions based on oblique references and the occasional date. And frankly, I liked spending time with Thunderbolt when he was nice.

My phone dinged. I looked down, texted back.

"Did you just make a date for sex?"

"I did. I kind of have to leave now."

"You shouldn't do this…"

"But I will."

I had a half hour to kill before Thunderbolt came over. I smoothed it over with a glass or two of wine. He had two modes, I think. 'Nice guy' and 'total ass.'

Thunderbolt: Be there in five.
Me: Okay.
Thunderbolt: In the Uber. Do you have condoms? Can stop if needed.
Me: Of course. I'm like a Girl Scout.
Thunderbolt: Good girl. Here.
Me: That was fast.
Thunderbolt: I live close.

When his 'here' text arrived, I wondered who in the hell would come to my front door. For the sex, which always featured the nice guy, I was kind of willing to take either beforehand.

Tonight I was in luck. It was 'nice guy.' He came through the door with a kiss and a smile.

I kind of wanted to know what had happened to that other guy who'd freaked out on me a few weeks back and sent a bunch of passive aggressive crazy texts after I admitted I'd met someone I liked. But I didn't ask.

Instead, I offered him a glass of wine. Then he brought his talking 'A' game. His movie premiere had gone well despite a last minute music clearance snafu. We talked far too long about everything and nothing, touching on penis euphemisms in romance a few too many times. A few glasses of wine in, they do get kind of funny.

Then he asked the question I wanted to avoid but couldn't.

"Tell me about Classic Car guy."

"There's nothing to tell. He's lovely."

"Lovely. You're going with that word."

I nodded.

"That's the most passive aggressive word, 'lovely.'"

I didn't exactly know what to say about the guy I liked, the guy who wasn't there. That we shared a similarly dysfunctional upbringing. That he was both strong and vulnerable at the same time. That when he was there with me, he was one hundred percent there. That when he was gone, it felt like he was a million miles away not twenty. Except, of course, he wasn't there this night.

Classic Car guy said he wanted to be with me, but he was always doing something else that was clearly more important to him. I was working overtime not to take that personally. Classic Car guy's words and actions, however, didn't quite match up. I didn't have the time to dedicate to figuring that piece out either. Or maybe it was that I didn't want to spend too much time figuring it out.

So I declared the topic of Classic Car guy off limits again, though Thunderbolt was happy to tell me stories about every person he'd seen since the last time I'd been with him, including a twenty-seven year old virgin he'd decided not to deflower.

After we killed a full bottle of wine, things got even better. He took my candles and arranged them on my nightstand so there was a soft glow in my bedroom. Then he undressed me slowly, reverently like it was a date instead of a hookup. For the first time, he didn't whisper what he wanted, but used his real voice to asked what I wanted. I gave him a list of the things I loved. Every item on my list got ticked.

What I got was a full two hours of screaming orgasms. He did any and everything he could to make sure that I was pleased. I'd like to say that I did my best in return. But all that wine may have clouded my memory of my reciprocation. I promised myself that I'd get him next time.

Right before I went to bed, after Thunderbolt had left and I'd blown out the candles, turned off the lights, and tucked myself into bed, I texted Day Trader to wish him well. Then I texted Classic Car guy.

Me: Off to bed. Hope you guys had fun. G'night. Also, there was wine. Lots of wine.

That was the most censored and measured text I'd ever sent in my life.

TWENTY

About to Jet Set

APRIL 5.

IN THE LAST MONTHS, I've thought my weekends should be titled, 'Waiting for Classic Car Guy.' Friday afternoon around two-thirty, he called.

"Honey, I have a few errands to run, then I'll head out your way."

Now for me, with a very tight relationship to time, that would mean I'd be at someone's house at three-thirty, maybe four. But I had to build in time for him, and I put his arrival at around six. He was seven minutes early. I was starting to get it.

Classic Car: I'm ready to eat, FYI. I'm hungry, sweetheart.
Me: Of course. Want to eat out or order in?
Classic Car: How about if you and I go out, stretch our legs?
Me: Okay. We'll Uber when you get here.
Classic Car: Is there a Korean barbecue near your place? I feel like some protein.
Me: Near...well, not too far, I have favorites.
Classic Car: How does Korean sound to you?

134

Me: Lovely, it's my favorite foreign cuisine.
Classic Car: No, it's not...
Me: What is?
Classic Car: A little birdie told me you have a sweet tooth for Salvadorian...

Which Classic Car guy was on his father's side. He had a way of being especially endearing when I least expected it.

I'll swear to you that from the moment he walked in, I had to try hard not to jump him. He'd just had six inches cut from his hair. It still ended well below his shoulders and suited him. But there was little that didn't suit him. In his nearly forty years, he'd earned a certain confidence.

I may have kissed him hello more than a few times at the back door before I ordered us an Uber to one of my favorite Korean barbecue joints and ushered him through my front door. We were really lucky because the wait for Korean barbecue on any night much less a Friday was usually well past a half hour, but tonight it was less than ten minutes.

After we were seated and the grill set to fire, Classic Car guy threw up his hands and professed to be a true Korean barbecue amateur.

"You order."

"What do you like?" Not that there were thousands of choices. I'd picked one of the better barbecues, but with a simple three item combo menu. Some of the higher end places featured dozens of meats in dazzling combinations. I was more interested in having a good time than feeding my foodie cred.

"Meat, chicken."

"Great. I'll pick something you'll love."

I ordered all pork, belly, collar, bean paste stew.

"So how are you?" he asked giving me what he would later call the Salvadoran stare. It wasn't so much a stare as it was a face open with interest in what I had to say. It was both heartwarming and discomfiting at the same time. It was like looking into the sun, but in a completely different way than when I was looking at Thunderbolt.

When Classic Car guy was looking at me across the table, I could see his adoration for me on his face, and I didn't know what to do with it. No one had ever really looked at me that way before in all my years. Romance heroines were really good, I thought, and accepting love. In real life, it wasn't so easy.

Sometimes I think I've become a tour guide into my world for Classic Car guy. He loved the food and was massively enthusiastic about it. The way he'd asked in the text, I really thought he had a love of Korean barbecue. Then I thought more about it, and it dawned on me.

I'd said a week or more back in my own text that I really loved Korean barbecue. It hadn't been the first time I'd talked about my love of Korean food, probably going back to that midnight run to the soon du bu tofu house. I realized that he wasn't so much out to please himself, but to please me. It worked very well.

He was in a walking and talking mood after dinner, so I did something I'd probably done never. We walked in Los Angeles. Our restaurant was on Sixth, so we hung a left and went south to Wilshire Boulevard. I'd driven on the street thousands of times, but it was fun experiencing life on foot. He held my hand or held me close everywhere we went. He was even so chivalrous as to move me closer when people were passing, or to switch sides when we encountered a careening man.

We didn't walk the whole way, but Ubered back the remaining two miles to my apartment. He took off his shoes and stacked them neatly by the door. I appreciated that he honored my preference for no shoes in my house. Though he'd been up since four AM, he still wanted to hang out a bit before turning in. I asked him what he wanted to watch, and he picked Netflix.

"Comedy?" I asked. We'd watched it before, and we both like stand up.

I flipped through a lot of people neither one of us wanted to see before I ended up on Kevin Hart.

"Yes or no?"

"You pick, honey. I think he's always entertaining."

"I watched his last special, and I don't quite get it. He's huge, one of the highest paid comedians, but his humor doesn't spark with me."

"I like the old guard best. Richard Pryor. Red Foxx. Early Eddie Murphy. George Carlin."

"Who doesn't?" I said. "But I don't think a lot of them are on Netflix."

I stopped talking and pressed play. Kevin Hart was entertaining, but after his hour, I was more interested in getting into bed.

After my last two conversations about sex with Thunderbolt, I was trying to pinpoint whether or not I wanted sex with Classic Car guy to be different. The bottom line was that Classic Car guy was not much into foreplay. A lot of kissing, a little touching, and he was always ready and eager to enter me.

It was weird, though, because from someone else, I'd really need more. More of everything. But there was something about him that got me hot and bothered just being within ten feet of him. I can only recall being that attracted to someone, and that had been when I was seventeen. After he entered me, though, he had amazing stamina. He could go a good ten minutes. That part felt amazing. Then not ten minutes after he came, he was ready to do it again, only the second time he always lasted even longer. I didn't know if it was fair to compare that to Thunderbolt's new 'A' game. For now, both worked.

Even breathing into my hair told me that Classic Car guy was drifting off. It was our first weekend together, and I'd been thinking about what we could do that would be fun. I kind of wanted to keep him in bed, like I'd threatened, but I kind of wanted to be out and about with him. I already knew he was fun at home.

After a big yawn, I turned my head so he could hear me.

"Would you like to go..." I started.

His breathing changed and I could feel his head shifting on the pillow.

"Go?"

"To the beach tomorrow?"

A big sigh huffed from his chest. "I thought you were asking me to leave..."

"No. Never," I said then turned and kissed him. This was the part I couldn't explain to Thunderbolt. What it was like caring for the feelings of someone who'd been asked to go one too many times in his life.

"The beach, yeah, that sounds like fun."

Between sex and showers and me whipping up a batch of chocolate chip banana muffins, it took us a bit to get to my car. We cruised to the beach down Santa Monica Boulevard.

Sometimes I forget that ninety percent of the people we encounter in the service industry speak Spanish. That's just the way it is in California for better or worse. Classic Car guy navigated in an entirely different world than I.

He spoke Spanish to everyone. The Uber drivers, the woman who gave us the tickets for beach parking, bussers, waiters, cleaners...everyone. I can speak Spanish, but rarely do. Usually only when necessary, when that's the only common language I share. The life he lives is slightly different than mine for a host of reasons, language among them.

We paid the exorbitant highway robbery parking fee the City of Santa Monica extorts as the weather warms, then we walked by the water all the way to Venice. He sought out some mural of Jim Morrison that he'd heard about, then we went to lunch.

My ex would have had lost his shit over lunch. Crowded beach seating, so-so service, and a quintessentially American menu would have pushed him over the edge from being a barely tolerable companion to me wanting to do whatever I could to rush things along and get back home where I could escape to the confines of my office.

Classic Car guy was the opposite. He did the thing he often did, switch around the chairs so that we were sitting closer together not across from each other.

We talked about everything and nothing. We shared food without controversy. He made me laugh. He made me feel cherished.

I took some lovely pictures of him that day. In front of that Jim Morrison mural and in front of a Burt Reynolds one from the Smokey and the Bandit era. He even took the best selfie of us. One I shared with all of my friends who said that I'd looked happier in that picture than they'd ever seen me. It's true. I look spectacular in that picture.

We'd happened on a drum circle in the Venice Beach sand. We stayed for an hour or so listening to the insistent drumbeat of amateurs coming together in rhythm.

"This is a beautiful thing," he said.

He was right. It was just the right tone for our last weekend together. Then his phone blew up. He wasn't one to answer, but today he did.

"What's going on?" I finally asked. Normally I didn't, but this was a lot even for him.

"I should tell you what's going on." His tone told me that what followed wasn't going to be good.

"Oh. Okay," I said. We were walking back from Venice, crossing over toward the Santa Monica pier. We sat for a second on one of the concrete benches along the strand.

"My ex has been hiding my kids."

I nodded. That explained a lot. He talked about them, but didn't see them that I could figure.

"Where?"

"Mexico, I think. I hired a private investigator. She says she's found them."

"That's huge."

"She wants me to come see her first thing in the morning."

Yes, I had the very selfish thought that our weekend was ending early. Obviously, I didn't express any of that. Instead we drove home while he talked about us having summer plans, going to festivals and the like. I always loved hearing this talk, but haven't ever believed it because he talks a good game but never makes a great plan. He'd taken a yearlong leave of absence from work, didn't have his kids with him, yet I was lucky to see him one day every couple of weeks. I was starting to realize that I wanted more from a relationship.

When we got to my place, he wrapped his arms around me and looked down at me.

"When are you going?" I asked. Though I knew the answer. My time with him was coming to a close. This twenty four hours was the longest I'd ever had.

"Now."

"I thought I could convince you to have a quickie," I said, only one percent joking.

"Can't, honey." Then we kissed a good long time. But no quickie was forthcoming. This man had boundaries of steel. He carefully packed his overnight bag and was gone before the sun was set.

I wanted him to be with his kids. That was important for both him and them, I assumed. Though, like his felony conviction, I thought there was probably a lot more to the story.

April 15.

After dealing with my accountant and my ex-husband, and e-filing our joint taxes in another time zone, I needed a breather. I propped up my iPad and opened Netflix. I was really touched to find a list of shows and comedy specials on 'My List.' Then I remembered an exchange Classic Car guy and I'd had after muffins.

"I'm going to jump in the shower really quickly, then we can go. Cool?" I'd asked.

"While you shower, can you show me how to operate the remote? I want to watch TV."

He'd never asked before, but I pointed to the relevant buttons and handed him the remote, not thinking too much about it.

When I was dressed, I came out to the living room. He was texting, and there wasn't anything happening on the screen.

"Did you find anything to watch?"

"No. Not really," he said, then powered off the set.

Until tax day, I hadn't thought about that exchange ever again. Not until I found all the shows I'd wanted to see conveniently at the top of the screen. During that last weekend together, I'd shared the same observation I'd mentioned to all of my friends.

Netflix had some great content...if you could find it. I never had the patience to find it. Classic Car guy had done it for me, though, found it and marked it. That was almost as good as a hot breakfast.

TWENTY-ONE

They're Just Not That Into Me

APRIL 21.

THE BEST THING about traveling a lot? I have friends all over the world. When one of my favorite author friends said, "Let's go to a writing conference in Italy," I said yes—nine months in advance. I knew that I'd be in the middle of a divorce. I had no idea what that would look like, but I said yes anyway.

So despite the logistics of navigating a divorce and temporary custody agreements, I flew to Italy and went to the conference. What can I say? Italy was wonderful.

I made friends with new authors and got to hang out with other authors I didn't see as often. I got to have genuine Italian prosecco and other lovely wines and pasta and such great food. I got to walk through cobblestone streets and take beautiful pictures of medieval buildings. I even took an hour out of my day to buy Classic Car guy the official Italian soccer jersey that he wanted.

In the two weeks I was away, though, I had a lot of time alone to think. Long plane rides and even longer walks through various European cities will do that to a writer.

The conclusion of all this thinking?

None of the guys I'm dating is that into me.

Not. A. Single. One.

A few weeks ago, I was looking at the stack of relationship and dating books a friend had sent. There sat probably three thousand pages of advice. Occasionally, I'd flip through one or another, but I didn't have the wherewithal to delve into any of it.

I could already conclude that reading all those pages wasn't going to answer the question of what I was looking for, how to figure out what I was looking for, whether or not I could find it once I figured it out, or how to identify the 'it' if I found it.

Then a little niggle started in the back of my head. I remembered seeing Greg Behrendt on Oprah. He and Liz Tuccillo were promoting their book, *He's Just Not That Into You.* It came out during the feverish time dating and sex were on everyone's minds as we tuned in to *Sex and the City* weekly.

While I was trying to unsnarl all of this dating in my mind, I realized that I needed to read that book. I'd never read it because I'd been married—to someone who wasn't that into me. I realized I needed to request it from the library because I had zero idea what I was doing this time around. I was free-wheeling, and it wasn't feeling all that good.

During my layover before flying back to California, I got a notification that the public library was happily lending me the audiobook I'd put on hold on a whim—*He's Just Not That Into You.* I downloaded it while on airport Wi-Fi and started listening while waiting for my boarding call.

A mere hour in, and it was like a veil had been lifted from my eyes.

The universe had put this in front of me at precisely the right time. Because I'd had a furious texting session with Classic Car guy on Thursday. Midnight for me. The middle of the afternoon for him. He'd had some kind of emergency hearing to try to gain back custody of his children. I knew we weren't in the kind of relationship where we shared those kinds of things in detail, but I was worried about him none-theless. He'd been unusually silent. From someone who sent flirty texts a few times most days, it was out of character.

I was even having stress dreams about him being in court where I woke up in a panic. I hate stress in my own life. I did not want to think about stress in someone else's.

To diffuse my own catastrophic thinking, I reached out and we texted a bit about the stuff that was stressing us out.

I'm going to be honest about the social mask I wear. I try to be the good time girl. I have a lot of stress of my own with divorcing someone abusive, sharing custody with that same person who hasn't changed. I have my share of guilt and sadness and having to accept that I've lost time with my precious child because I had to leave a situation that was too emotionally scarring to endure any longer. I save discussions about all that for my therapist and best friends.

But it's hard keeping up that façade all the time outside of those confessionals, and I let it slip twice in front of Classic Car guy. The first the night I landed, he called me on Face-Time, having just stepped out of the shower. He propped the phone up against his pillows and lay on his very naked stomach while making me laugh and looking sexy while doing it.

It was the first time I'd traveled abroad without my son since he'd been born, really, and I was having a hell of a time smiling while I had to contend with the utter quiet that comes when there aren't children. I think I almost cried for a moment before pulling it back together, getting that social mask back up.

None of that is important, though, to my revelation. What I realized after texting furiously, more than a week after I'd left, was that he's not that into me. Whether it's his custody situation, or his search for the perfect car, or perfect car parts, or his physical therapy for a torn rotator cuff (been there done that, still had time for a life), or his sister, or his nephews, or, or, or...I'm not that important in his life, and I think I wanted to be. I told him that point blank. His response:

Radio silence.

I now realize what I want. I want a guy who can't wait to see me. Who comes over when he says he will. Who calls when he says he will. Who even texts when he promises to. Someone for whom one overnight every other week isn't enough. Who doesn't think a few miles are a barrier that can't be overcome.

I know that in many ways Classic Car guy gives all the signs of someone who wants to be in a relationship, but it's a false assumption on my part, because signaling isn't enough to turn it into reality.

My plane lands in Los Angeles at seven on a Monday night. If he was into me, he'd want to know that. I wouldn't have to remind him. So I'm not—going to remind him, that is. I'm landing and that next day I'll pick up my son, the most precious person in my life, and spend the next two weeks with him. The beauty of having a child is that dating is off the table when he's with me as it should be at this stage.

While I'm alone, like I've been for these couple of weeks in Europe, I've just looked back through the texts since Thursday, and you know what? It's me, reaching out, sending pictures, trying to cajole a text, a reaction, something from him.

And it's exhausting.

It's exhausting trying to make plans. Don't get me wrong. He's sexy as hell, and sweet, and kind and when he's with me, kissing me, holding my hand, making me breakfast, setting up Netflix, and making love with me—I feel it—loved. To get to those times feels like sledding uphill, though.

There is someone else out there. I'm sure of it. Someone else who is kind and sexy as well, that is. I just haven't met him yet.

After I land, that means good-bye to Day Trader. What is that about? Great conversation? A fun companion for shopping at Erewhon? I want someone who can't keep his hands off of me. Good bye to Mr. Irish. I don't even like him that much. And as my friend who met him pointed out, he didn't even put on nice clothes to see me.

The only person I'm keeping around is Thunderbolt. He's the most honest of them all. He wants uncomplicated sex. I want uncomplicated sex. I'm going to text him now before this plane takes off for my eleven-hour flight home because I want to have uncomplicated sex when I land with someone who's exactly who he says he is and shows up when he says he's going to. What does it say that he's the most straightforward I've encountered?

TWENTY-TWO

Mr. Music

MAY 5.

IT'S BEEN a long week since I've been back from Italy. The minute I landed Classic Car Guy started texting like he had nothing better to do with his thumbs. This from a man who asked me to send him pictures of my first trip to Italy. To tell him all about the food and architecture. To share snippets of my life with him.

I did all that. I took walks, I snapped a picture. Sent it.

I ate beautiful fresh food with friends, I snapped a picture. Sent it.

He responded to the first few, and that warmed me. There, I thought, now we have the regular back and forth that I think couples should have.

Of course, I spun all of that out into a greater fantasy. Maybe one day he could travel with me and we could share these kinds of experiences together. Or maybe we'd have the kind of relationship where I could give him my flight info and he'd pick me up from the airport, whisk my bags from baggage claim, and have a sexy fun reunion that would make me forget all about the awful jet lag a nine hour time difference can bring.

Lovely fantasy.

Wrong guy.

I had a two -day layover in London before coming back to Los Angeles.

Me: I have some downtime before I get back to Los Angeles. If you want to FT or talk, we can connect anytime.

More silence.

At some point I would have to acknowledge that he's ignoring me. That he's decided that he's not even going to read the messages on his phone from me. For a man practically attached to his phone, and a second phone he sometimes carries, that's a high level of ghosting.

I mean I honestly don't get it. It's all, "I want you. I miss you. Let's go away for the weekend." Then nothing. Only silence.

It's like he had a sixth sense that I was back in the U.S.

Monday: You're home? Can you talk?

We talked. He didn't apologize for his absence. That's not his way. Instead, he offered lunch for Wednesday or Thursday.

Tuesday: *sends head and chest pic*
Wednesday: *sends picture of himself cooking* *sends pic of his deceased father*
Thursday: Honey, I'm a little backed up. Doesn't look like I can make it. Friday is better. *sends picture of himself grilling*
Friday: Morning honey. I've been here with my doctors taking a new MRI. Shoulders/back not doing

well. I'm going to be here a while... Not ignoring you
FYI. I miss you.

Then lots of sexy texting. How he wants to spend hours
exploring each other. Though I have to say that taking it slow
was not his specialty. I think he's what I'd call a penis-centric
guy. He thinks that as long as he can maintain an erection (or
six), he doesn't have to do anything more.

Even though he claimed that weekends were hard, he
couldn't see me when I got back and offered up weekdays.
That weekend I was with my son while my ex went away to
Paris.

So all that buildup. All that sexting.

Then radio silence.

I liked him a lot. He was cute. And...I was going to say nice
and considerate, but I wasn't sure if that was true. I think he
was those things in person.

But talking about making plans, then never making good
on those plans, probably canceled out the nice and considerate
part of the equation. That left me with really freaking sexy.
That was a trait I liked. It would have been better on a
friends-with-benefits relationship and not on a guy who
claimed to want a relationship but was doing nothing to start,
maintain, or grow one.

Because I wanted that and wasn't getting it from him, I
was ninety percent sure I was going to break up with him
when I (finally) saw him and gave him his souvenirs from Italy.
I didn't count on not being able to see him to tell him I didn't
want to see him anymore.

Oh, the irony.

I was halfway between taking the clothes I bought for him
back to Europe with me and returning them or keeping them
for myself. If I heard from him, I guessed I'd ask him for his
address (probably said something that I didn't have it) then

send the stuff on along with some of the stuff he left at my apartment.

Back on the dating market I went, not that I'd ever really gone off.

This week was Mr. Music. I'd actually connected with Mr. Music before I left for Italy back at the beginning of April.

You know how it went. His picture on Tinder was cute. He had long curly hair. He played music. I swear if Tinder had a filter for that, I could save a shit ton of time swiping left on all the doctors, lawyers, and accountants in their pinstripe suits holding bottles of champagne, glasses of scotch or the bonnets of their hundred thousand dollar cars.

Mr. Music: Hi Jolie, this is me, Mr. Music.
Me: Good morning.
Mr. Music: Good morning, beautiful.

Okay, he was going to be one of these; the kind who thought that paying me compliments would get me into bed. It had worked for Classic Car guy. Thunderbolt hadn't even tried. Both approaches could be equally successful.

I was easy.

Either way, I hadn't been able to meet up with Mr. Music in person before I went to Italy.

I think we hadn't gotten together because he'd had his teenage daughter at home for a couple of weeks. I'd had my sick kid home on another weekend. And probably Classic Car guy. I'd probably given up a definite date for the possibility of Classic Car guy.

I wasn't doing that anymore. So while Classic Car guy was texting me daily about his custody problems and the many solutions he was spinning out in his head to solve them, I was making plans on Saturday.

Mr. Music: Jolie, are you in LA yet?

Me: I'm here. Almost over jet lag as well. I've had my kid since I've landed. He's back with his dad this weekend, however...

Mr. Music: Really?? Do you have some time on Sunday to meet? What part of LA are you in?

Me: Sunday would be great. I'm in West Hollywood. Where are you?

Mr. Music: Near Sepulveda and Washington. How about we meet at the Farmer's Market.

The Farmer's Market in Los Angeles is on the corner of Fairfax Avenue and Third Street. It used to be just that, a market where one could buy fresh produce.

It is also adjacent to CBS studios. They tape *The Price is Right* there among other live shows. On any given day, the contestants are lined up outside. They're easy to spot with their custom printed T-shirts.

Since I moved to Los Angeles, a large mall had been built next to the Farmer's Market, the Grove. It's your typical Los Angeles mall. Boring on the outside, looks like Disneyland on the inside, has a bunch of the usual chain stores. From West Hollywood, I can get there on foot, so on the whole it's not a bad place to meet. There are tons of restaurants and places where people can enjoy coffee.

Every month a group of romance author friends gets together and do a Zoom hangout online. It's a way to keep up with industry stuff and not get too isolated. I have a job where it's easy not to talk to people for hours or days at a time. Unlike most Sundays which are for yoga, on this one, I got up, pulled myself together and put on a cute sweater dress, tights, and ankle boots. Then I texted Mr. Music to make sure he'd show up. I hadn't been stood up yet, but neither had I met a great planner.

Me: I have a 90 minute conference call this morning ending at 11:30 that I'm prepping for. Let me know where you'd like to meet, and I'll be walking out the door the minute the call is done...

I was tired of figuring out when to meet, where to meet, what to do. I'd decided that the guy should put in more effort than driving.

Mr. Music: Cool. See you soon.
Me: My meeting just finished. On my way over. Where do you want to meet?
Mr. Music: I am down the street right now in traffic not too far away. As soon as I park, I'll start walking towards the Farmer's Market.
Mr. Music: Three blocks away...
Mr. Music: Parking.

You see what's missing here, right? A plan. If I'm so lovely, and gorgeous and beautiful—according to them—you'd think they'd try to put in some effort. I wasn't thinking I'd come across that guy yet, you know one willing to put in any work other than driving.

Me: I'm here.
Mr. Music: Me too. I'm at the Coffee Bean. It's on the north side.
Me: I'm not sure I knew there was a Coffee Bean here...

More logistics texting ensued as I weaved my way through lots of stores. But there it was, a coffee shop on the corner near the Farmer's Market entrance. I walked in, introduced myself, fully expecting him to offer to buy me a cup of coffee.

Nope.

Instead, he offered to sit at one of the hundreds of outside picnic tables at the market where patrons hang out eating food from one of the many establishments.

I'm not going to say it was a case of bait and switch. I'll merely say the pictures he posted were from another decade entirely. He was at least fifteen years older and a lot heavier than his pictures. If these were his 'make an effort' clothes, I'd hate to know what his lay around and not make an effort clothes looked like.

He was in a faded band T-shirt. I've forgotten the band. Jeans. Sneakers.

In my cute dress, styled hair, and those black leather ankle boots, I felt...overdressed. Like I was trying hard and he wasn't trying at all.

Without water or coffee or tea, I sat at the Farmer's Market and asked him questions about himself. His daughter was sixteen. They were going car shopping the next weekend. He was an audio engineer. Long story short when singers, bands, and musicians were recording music, he was in charge of recording and mixing. I think that all added up to making sure it sounded good. On the side he'd recently taken on fixing the sound on podcasts as well.

He also made his own music, though he didn't offer up any samples. Instead, he talked about his divorce and the moves he'd made between Los Angeles and Massachusetts as he tried and failed to save his marriage and family.

I stayed for maybe two hours. I'll spare you the rest of the conversation because it wasn't that interesting. Although he did give me a link to a YouTube video my son did enjoy that was a spoof of Power Rangers, so there's that.

When I let him hug me goodbye, he seemed like he was sad to see me go. I was glad to leave, to get some to go sushi for lunch at the health food store on the corner, and catch up with a friend by phone on the walk home.

A couple of days later I received a text.

Mr. Music: Hello Jolie, I must say you are even prettier in person than your photos.

Yup, I've heard that one before. I still maintain that the photos are pretty good. If I'm a pleasant surprise, I won't change them. For a moment I thought about responding. But I put as much effort into my response as he put into planning a date. Which was: none.

TWENTY-THREE

Vulnerabilities

MAY 10.

CLASSIC CAR GUY'S special ringtone sounded. His face appeared on FaceTime.

"You're free?" he asked with a knowing smile. I could fall into that smile.

My "Yes." probably came back before he'd even finished his last breath.

"I'm just driving past downtown. I'm going to see a guy about painting my car, then I'll swing by your place."

"Can't wait."

My heart sang. I closed my laptop and did a little dance around my apartment. Then I texted a friend of mine. A fellow author who's also going through a divorce with kids. We traded advice. She helped me navigate divorce stuff. I helped her navigate dating stuff. Her parting shot: enjoy him.

"I missed you, honey," were his first words as he came up through my back door. I hugged him a good long time.

"So good to see you," I said.

"I also missed that couch of yours," he said as he pulled me through the hall to the living room. We fell onto the gray leather cushions. I flicked at a white spot in the middle of his black V-neck. "What's this?"

His laugh was hearty. "Toothpaste. At least I tried," he said.

Then he kissed me and we stopped talking. When it was obvious that we were done talking, we moved from the living room to my bedroom. There's something about time, and distance, and perspective that made this hard to fall into, to enjoy.

When he was satisfied, I got up and off and took a shower. Then he did. When he came out fully dressed, he announced he was hungry.

"Do you have time? Before you pick up your son from school?"

I looked up at the clock. There was plenty of time. I took him down to a Thai restaurant within walking distance of my apartment. Then my phone started ringing off the hook. That abusive ex I try to avoid was throwing a tantrum and making a mess that my lawyers were busy trying to clean up. I couldn't ignore them. So I stepped out of the restaurant and took the call—for ten long minutes.

"Sorry about that. Lawyers."

I don't know how to get through the awkward times with people. I didn't want to talk about how we weren't gelling just then, so I asked what he was doing that was keeping him so busy; (the 'so busy he couldn't see me' part went unspoken).

He talked about his sister, whom he drove two hours to see nearly daily. He talked about how he was planning to be this incredible father once he had time with his kids again. He was thinking of moving to Riverside or San Diego so that he could pop in and see his kids for an hour here and an hour there. Maybe he'd buy a house in San Bernardino.

He had a lot of thoughts. A lot of plans. I didn't begrudge him those plans, but I didn't really see how we could have any sort of relationship when his priorities lay several counties away. I didn't say that, of course, because cool girls don't point out the obvious.

He was in an affectionate mood, so we held hands while we walked the long way back to my apartment.

Once inside, I prompted him to sit. I stuck my head in my bedroom closet and pulled out the gifts I'd brought back from Italy in April. It was the soccer jersey that he'd asked for. The one he'd texted me pictures of. The other was a jersey from my favorite country.

"These are for you," I said thrusting the bag at him. I'm shit at wrapping presents even though I love giving gifts.

"For me?" he asked his eyes full of surprise.

"You asked. I delivered," I said.

He took them out his face filling with delight.

"You didn't have to do this. I didn't expect you to do this."

I melted at that. How could this man not think himself worthy of my thought and consideration? I hugged him, then my phone alarm buzzed. Writing can make me lose track of time, so I have an alarm on my phone to make sure I don't forget to pick up my son from school. We both headed out my back door. Once we were at the cars, he grabbed me and kissed me hard.

Then he hesitated a moment and looked at a long scar that I have on my elbow.

"What's that?" he said tracing the puckered flesh with his finger.

I took a deep breath doing everything I could to keep the tears back. When my son had asked me this question when he was two or three, I'd answered honestly. I'd answered honestly every other time my son had asked. But I'd never answered the question when anyone else had asked. I blinked away the tears and I told the truth.

"My ex pushed me down the second year we were married.

I fell backwards on the concrete driveway and my elbow split open. He said it was my fault."

Classic Car guy bent down and kissed the scar, then kissed me. Without any other words we both got in our cars and pulled away.

After eight that night, he texted me.

Classic Car: Would your ex do that to you often?
Me: Often? Not really. My life was all yelling and threats and dangerous driving. I chose to stay way too long and that's on me. But the behavior continues, only from 10 miles away.
Classic Car: Funny how men do that shit to women but NEVER pick a fight with a random man...
Me: I know...
Classic Car: Anything ever happens, you call me.
Me: Didn't want my kid living like that
Classic Car: I'm sorry to hear that.
Me: The last weeks are on me. He's prohibited from contact with me except under very limited circum-stances, but I needed to guarantee I could get my kid on a plane. Had to do more than an hour call to get that secured so I didn't get pulled at the airport...
Classic Car: Now I understand your worries while you were away. You need anything I'm here.

TWENTY-FOUR

Thunderbolt turns up...again.

"WHAT ARE you looking for in a relationship?" I was looking straight at Thunderbolt as I asked this question.

He cocked his head and looked at me funny. This was the first time he'd ever sat on my couch. I'm going to be honest. The couch is legendary. Everyone who comes to my apartment comments on it. Friends have fantasized about all girl sleepovers we could have on the couch.

Up until now, I'd entertained Thunderbolt in my kitchen. We'd have water or wine, kiss, talk for an hour or three, then eventually get to the bedroom. Today, he asked for permission to sit on the couch.

I acquiesced.

"I'm asking because people keep asking me, and I have no idea what in the hell to answer," I continued.

I'd just changed my dating profile from "something casual" to "I don't know yet," because I had changed. In these few months I realized that I might want more than casual sex. It wasn't that I was against casual sex, because there's a lot to be said for it. It's that the effort was outweighing the reward. It was that having spent time with Classic Car, I realized there were certain aspects of our relationship that I really enjoyed and wanted more of.

Someone thinking of me morning and night and checking in to see how I was. Someone who remembered little things about me. Someone who enjoyed being with me. Someone who held my hand in public and didn't walk a quarter mile in front of me like I had a disease they needed to be quarantined from.

"I want to find someone who's funny, enjoys sex, and is independent," Thunderbolt answered after a long pause.

"How will you know?" I asked. My armchair observation was that he'd probably encountered that woman a million times but had walked right by her while he was waiting for the heavens to open up and give him a sign. I didn't share that, though. He'd have to pay his own therapist for that one.

"I know when I won't," he answered cryptically.

"What do you mean?"

"A couple of months ago, I met this girl I liked. We went on a couple of dates. Then one day she texted me in the middle of the afternoon."

The middle of the afternoon didn't seem like a crime against humanity. I was enjoying my middle of the afternoon texts, but this made me curious.

"So..." I prompted.

"So she was completely blitzed. She wanted me to come over to her house and who knows what? But she was nearly black out drunk in the middle of the day. I told her that I wasn't coming over because I was working. She'd have to wait until later when I was done working. That was the last time I talked to her."

I'm not sure what I was expecting, but that wasn't it. Black out drunk during the middle of the day would certainly be a deal breaker for me and probably most sane people. I didn't have a comeback for that one. Couldn't defend that woman who sounded like she might be a mess. Nothing like the twenty-seven year old virgin of a few weeks ago that he'd decided not to deflower. That virgin, I think, may have appreciated the effort.

"Speaking of relationships? How's yours?" he asked, his gaze intent.

"And we're back," I said with a flourish of my hand what I hoped was a heavy dose of frustration in my voice. "Suffice it to say, it's crazy. Do you want kids?" I asked turning the focus back on him. I had friends. I had a therapist. I did not need to download my issues with Classic Car guy during our time together. There was enough of that already with my girl-friends. I think I spent more hours talking *about* him than *to* him

"If I meet this perfect woman and it's part of the package, then I'd do it."

"Hmm." It took all the self -restraint I'd built up over my long life not to cough or comment on his use of the word 'per-fect.' If he'd said 'perfect for me' that would have been accept-able, but there was no perfect woman. Woe to this one. If I were a betting women, I'd have wagered on the side of him not finding her—ever.

"How do you like the drink?" He pointed to the white and pink can of what I thought to be flavored seltzer in his hand. He was odd that way, bringing over random drinks of the alco-holic and non -alcoholic variety. I'd opened it, and taken a few sips. But caught up in black -out drunken tales and a laser focus on the word perfect, I hadn't been paying attention to what I'd been putting in my mouth.

"Is it grapefruit?"

"Taste it. You tell me."

I took a sip, realized I'd just brushed my teeth and adjusted for that. "It is."

"You said you liked grapefruit and seltzer, so I brought it for you."

That descended into a discussion of LaCroix which is the most popular thing in Los Angeles right now after Teslas and trying to get a show on Netflix.

I don't know how long we spent gabbing about his work and mine and of course his documentary. It was only when he took the can from my hand and kissed me that I realized I was probably way too passive.

Despite all my texting and summoning him, he always had to make the first move. It was the opposite of how it was with Classic Car guy. After those first two dates, I felt like I was nearly always all over him. But this moment wasn't a time for comparison. Instead, I let Thunderbolt undress me and lead me to my bedroom.

There may have been no future, and maybe not even anything to our relationship. But for goodness sake, the sex was good. It was better every single time. I was gaining a deep appreciation for a guy who tried hard (and succeeded) at pleasing me and was always on time.

TWENTY-FIVE

The Revelation

MAY 26.

Thunderbolt: I'm back today if you wanna get together tonight.
Me: From Where? Just left yoga. Definite maybe. Let me get home first.

I GOT that text at 12:35. I'd left my phone in my car because otherwise it would have buzzed my smartwatch and totally taken me out of the Zen of yoga.

I needed that Zen. When I'd gotten in my car after one PM, there were other texts waiting...from Classic Car...that had arrived exactly at the same time: 12:35. Must have been some magic hour when the universe put me in the mind of two different guys.

By now, you know how this was likely to go. Classic Car guy will say something endearing and heartwarming that will totally pull me back in. Will he be available, though? Likely not. Thunderbolt was always my second choice, but he was consistent, and on time, and always there when he said he would be.

So I left it. Drove the ten minutes home. Lugged my farmer's market haul and empty water bottle up to my kitchen.

I looked at my phone.

Spun around my kitchen.

Went into my utility room.

Cleaned the lint out of my dryer.

Heaved a big sigh.

Then made a decision.

Thunderbolt: Back from Orlando.

Me: I'm in. Time?

Thunderbolt: 9?

Me: That works. See you later the.

Me: *then. Whatevs with the autocorrect.

I put down the phone and felt crushing guilt. I'd never felt that before at any time I'd seen Thunderbolt. I'm the author of the chapter in the first installment of this little dating memoir, 'It's not cheating of there's no commitment.'

Up until this moment it had been all about my agency. About spending time with a guy I liked, but didn't 'like, like' because the sex was good, the companionship was good, and he was physically if not emotionally available.

But my friend was right. He was the TGIUTAFATOG (the guy I use to avoid feelings about the other guy). Something about all that felt disingenuous and wrong -headed. The previous Friday another friend, a devout Christian, had been over.

She'd been ringside to these dates the past few weeks, and she was rooting for Classic Car guy. She thought I should see only him. So what if he was available only two nights a month...that would be enough for her, she'd said.

Not that I'm judging, but my devout Christian friend was the poster girl for unavailable. Nearly twelve years after her own divorce, her ex had remarried. His son was born only a few days after my own. But she was still bitter about him leaving and wasn't quite ready to date, though quality men buzzed around her like flies. I didn't want what she had, a couple of dates a month that were destined to go nowhere.

That kind of thing wasn't enough for me. I didn't realize it wasn't until I was falling half in love with someone who disappeared when he got overwhelmed by feelings.

I couldn't figure out why there was guilt about choosing Thunderbolt over him. So I just lived with that feeling, for a few hours until it all but disappeared with the sound of the text tone a few minutes before nine.

Thunderbolt: Getting ready to head over.
Me: Okay.
Thunderbolt: Here.

And he was here in my apartment like clockwork as always. He showed up.

It started the exact same way it always started. I asked Thunderbolt how he was. He remarked on how clean my apartment was. I offered him wine. He took a stool at my breakfast bar.

"So about that guy you're seeing?" *That* was his opening gambit.

"Why are we back on that third rail of conversation again?" I asked. I thought we'd established during that first date that he did not want a relationship.

I was in one, just with someone else. So I didn't have a clue as to why he gave two shits about the other guy. He didn't want what the other guy had—my full attention.

"I really don't care. But you can tell me," he said in the two most contradictory sentences to be spoken in my apartment that day.

The "really not caring" part of his speech did not at all match up with his "so what about that guy" part of his speech. So I told him an extremely edited version of Classic Car's story. I moved the salt shaker to one side of my black granite counter.

"He said on his profile that there was no drama." I lifted the shaker, the rock salt making a sound like beans in castanets. Let's say that this salt is no drama." I lifted the pepper shaker and shifted it about three feet from its salt companion, its multicolor corns giving off a different sound. "This pepper is drama of the highest order."

He nodded.

I pointed toward the cabinet way to the far side of the pepper shaker. "He's over there in the drama department. Varsity level. I sent a sexy text. Twelve hours later, I get pictures of his kids. No words. I had no idea what in the hell to say to that."

Thunderbolt's eyebrows shot up the way mine probably had when I literally got a response text of Classic Car with the two children he hadn't seen in over a year. Then we moved on to something else, mainly a download of his trip to Orlando doing a gig for ESPN.

"Wait, you came back from Orlando today?" I asked genuinely confused.

"Yep. I got up at four AM for the flight. Upgraded for more room."

"Where did you text me from?" I asked because last time I checked TSA and all those post 9/11 rules barred us from texting on planes.

"The plane. How amazing is technology that you can text for sex from thirty thousand feet?"

(For the protection of Thunderbolt's identity and to save him from federal prosecution, I'm just going to assume that the plane had free Wi-Fi.)

"It is amazing," I agreed.

There was wine.

More wine.

Spilled wine (me).

Cleaning it up (him).

Then we took the party to my bedroom.

We were in that part where the clothes were coming off as fast as they could. He put a stack of condoms on my side table. It was the first time he'd brought them. I didn't know what to make of that show of responsibility, so I closed my eyes and took in the pleasure.

"If you want, we can do it without a condom," he said between kisses.

My "I'm sorry?" was an invitation to repeat what he'd just said. I have to admit that one, I lose my ability to think clearly when someone is kissing me, and two, I was ninety percent sure I'd misunderstood him.

"I was just tested."

I swear to god it was like I'd been tossed into some romance novel where the hero talked about having been tested and suddenly condoms go by the wayside. But you know, without the romance and happily ever after.

"Not tonight," I demurred. I'd honestly have to think about it. The number of times I'd had sex without a condom could be counted on one hand. Well that was before the divorce because it was only the few times necessary to conceive my son. If we throw in that first night, you know the five or six times with Classic Car guy, then it was a full two hands for sure, but still not a lot. After that I'd been tested because while Classic Car guy was cute (oh FFS, sexy as all get out) and nice, I didn't know him well enough to trust that he was disease free.

Then we stopped talking. It's as if Thunderbolt is in a contest with himself. Every time he comes over, he's got more tricks up his sleeve. Our first time together was tame in comparison to this night. This was let your freak flag fly sex. It was equal parts amazingly satisfying and exhausting. I appreciated the exhausting part because it would let me sleep long and hard later.

The orgasms he gave me kept away that middle of the night insomnia where I reread Classic Car guy's texts and rehashed the moments we'd been together looking for clues about what he really thought or felt. He claimed to be an open book, but it felt like he constantly riffled those pages and I never really got to see anything.

"You know what?" Thunderbolt said into the silence where I was processing my secretly non-monogamous guilt and he was dozing.

"What?"

"You're funny and delightful." He yawned then turned toward me.

I didn't have to respond because in seconds he was asleep. The extra three hours of awake time and athletic sex had done him in.

It was funny because in all these months I've never seen him sleep. I left him to it. He was exhausted. I lay on my back watching the ceiling fan twirl. It was my ex's birthday. Thunderbolt had gotten my ex's annual birthday blowjob.

"I've never fallen asleep before. That was weird," he said when he woke up an hour later.

"I wasn't going to murder you in your sleep, so you're all good."

"When are you traveling again?" he asked me.

"June."

"And you're gone for the whole summer?"

"I told you this last week," I said kind of matter-of-factly. "You're traveling to Korea and Aspen and maybe Italy. So you'll be gone as well."

I wasn't sure why in the hell he was concerned with my summer plans. I never spent the summer in Southern California. Probably a legacy of people fleeing the hot, humid swelter that was New York City when I was a kid.

Summers were for...well...summering. And I didn't do it the city that was already in perpetual summer. I liked a change of scenery when school wasn't in session.

"Why would you want to have sex without a condom?" I asked. "I've only done that about four times in my life," I added. That was true. Or the statement would have been true before I met Classic Car guy. For him, I'd totally abandoned my principles. For some reason I trusted him but verified. According to UCLA Health I was clean.

"Seriously?" he asked open -mouthed. A friend of mine suggested that the minute a man got an erection, his prefrontal cortex (the part of the brain that does the reasoning, has the judgment, etc.) goes offline.

For Thunderbolt, who I imagine was having, and had already had all sorts of indiscriminate sex across many states, not thinking that protecting himself from disease and—you know—unplanned pregnancies was paramount made me wonder.

"When I wanted to get pregnant. And that first time with the other guy. It's why I got tested in March. How often do you get tested?"

"Twice a year."

"So? Sex without a condom?" I really wanted to hear one of these excuses in person. I'd heard them all on the Savage Love-cast. Though I'm pretty sure Dan Savage had pulled out the results of some study that said that the idea that there was sensation loss with condoms had mostly been debunked.

"It's more intimate somehow. Sex is more organic without."

I took a long pause trying to figure out why he'd want to be more intimate—with me. Every other action that this man took practically screamed, *I don't want intimacy.* The people pleaser in me spoke up before the rational side of my brain could step in.

"Well, if you want to do it without a condom next time, that would be fine." Because apparently my own prefrontal cortex had gone offline. Or maybe I wanted more intimacy too. Before that thought could go anywhere, I shut that shit down.

"Next time then." He yawned big. "Oh, okay. I should get going."

Then he gathered up all his stuff, hailed his Uber or Lyft and left. And I went to bed. Slept like a baby—no worries about Classic Car guy. To be honest, I was reliving the great sex, and he wasn't even a thought in my mind until the next morning.

I got up early to hit the gym. While I was working out, I had world's biggest revelation, because maybe sweating brings a brain back online in the exact opposite way sex takes it offline.

Anyway, my huge revelation: Classic Car guy says he's available, but he's not. Thunderbolt says he's not, but he is, or he really wants to be.

Also, I needed to get the hell out of town for the summer.

TWENTY-SIX

The Break-up

JUNE 4.

AFTER GATHERING ALL MY COURAGE, and working this out in the Notes app on my phone, I sent the following text to Classic Car guy at 7:28 AM in the morning.

Me: Writing this over text is the last thing I want to do but maybe the easiest. Hard things should always be said in person. Unfortunately I don't see us getting that chance. I want to make your life easier, not harder. I'm not sure I'm doing that. You are a lovely and delightful person. I'm so glad to have met you, especially at this time when my life has been in the middle of so many big changes. I think it's best if we stop seeing each other. Although to be honest, I guess you have already made that decision. We just haven't talked about it. I do hope that your upcoming move goes well and that you have the time and opportunity to reconnect with your beautiful children. Wishing you a great summer ahead as well.
xo Jolie

YES, I'll agree that breaking up with a guy via text wasn't ideal. May have even been tacky. But how had Classic Car guy left me with any real choice? Our relationship could be summed up with three kinds of text exchanges.

No.1:
Me: Let's make a plan.
Him: Sends hawt photo. *doesn't make a plan*

No. 2:
Me: Are we getting together this weekend?
Him: Yes, let me run an errand and get back to you in a couple of hours.
Him: *radio silence for three days*

OR, as Monty Hall would have said...

No. 3:
Him: Hey sweetheart. I can't wait to spend the weekend with you, go dancing with you, eat out with you, go to Mexico with you.
Me: Yes, yes, and yes.
Him: *radio silence for three or more days*

NONE of those three scenarios ended up with me getting what I wanted.
A relationship with him.
Time with him.
Intimacy with him.
Sex with him.

Him.

By June, after all of those scenarios had played themselves out more times than I could count, I was more interested in saving my sanity than seeing him in person. So I sent that text. Then I went out for a full day retreat with some fellow romance authors and dear friends who help keep me sane in my writing and personal life.

Five and a half hours later, while we were in the middle of discussing writing, marketing, and the obstacles holding us back from greater success, my phone trilled with his special ring tone (iPhone's 'Descent' if you're wondering). The one I sometimes heard in my sleep while I was waiting for him to show up but it was always a dream.

> **Classic Car:** Actually I'm sorry you feel that way.
> There's a lot of drama going on actually, didn't feel that
> you should be dealing with any of it. I'm sorry to have
> bothered.

Seriously, I thought. That was his response. The guy who said he'd had no drama now had drama but was sorry to have bothered me. I never thought I was a people pleaser, but for some reason I didn't want *him* to feel bad even though he'd made me feel bad every single day he had promised to see me and didn't show. So I sent another message the next morning at seven. Yes, I know this wasn't good or sane, but I couldn't help myself.

> **Me:** Probably my biggest flaws are that I talk too much
> and don't know when to stop talking. For some reason I
> really don't want you to misunderstand me. Which is
> why I'm sending this text when I really need to make
> breakfast for that kid and should really put down this
> phone. But see earlier re: flaws. I'm really going to miss

you fiercely. I already have. Honestly, I'm crying as I type this. I get that you have drama. That's not it. It's that I felt like you just shut me out. I try really hard to maintain a 'cool girl' facade. And I think I'm good at it. But to be frank it hurt a lot when you went silent. I'm mature enough not to take it too personally. But at some point, it's hard to wait and hope and wait and then realize that you're just not going to be there. I never wanted to feel like I was pestering you because I never wanted to be something else on your 'to do' list. But it got too hard for me to have all these feelings for you and...I don't know. I think I'm writing this because we both had/have(?) the crazy mom problem, and I don't want you to feel minimized or unseen or what-ever. But I think I don't want to feel that way either and that's what happened.

From him no response, though the read receipt popped up instantly. Of course he wasn't going to respond. What would he say to all of that? Sorry, in the true, genuine, apologetic way, wasn't in his vocabulary. I closed my phone, got my kid ready, took him to school while making cheerful small talk about Minecraft or who the fuck knows what.

Then I got home and cried.

For three days.

Not sure why I was so sad. I think I missed the idea of what could have been. Not what was. Not being stood up and ignored and forgotten.

One friend sat with me during a breakfast of oatmeal in the middle of one of those open plan restaurants as I cried.

Another sat with me through dim sum where I'd had my date with The Aussie and watched me cry. She was kind enough to bring me peonies.

I did spinning.

I did yoga.

I meditated.

I cried.

I had to have my friends keep me on the phone to keep me from texting, but I did it, I held fast even though I was crying the whole time.

TWENTY-SEVEN

Like clockwork

Thunderbolt: Are you still in LA?
Me: I am. Just doing the usual Sunday yoga.
Thunderbolt: Nice.

I DIDN'T HAVE the patience for the usual dance. Where he asked all sorts of oblique questions that were all variations of 'when can we next have sex?' So I cut to the chase.

Me: Until Thursday. If you're game, I'm extending an invite for tonight...
Thunderbolt: Cool. If I can wrap up work, I'm down.
Me: LMK. I'm writing while at the car wash which is all kinds of nutso LA behavior.

Eight hours later...

Me: I'm quitting work for the night. Out of ideas...for my Chinese billionaire. You?
Thunderbolt: I could swing by.
Me: OK. Maybe you have Chinese billionaire ideas...

Thunderbolt: Sure. I'll be there at 10:04
Me: That's oddly precise.
Thunderbolt: Quoting the Lyft app.
Me: LOL.
Thunderbolt: Here.

And he was, here in my too clean apartment that is. He looked at my clock as I invited him through the front door. It was exactly four after ten. He pointed that out and smiled.

He took off his shoes, made himself at home. Hung something on one of my hooks. Borrowed a bottle opener from my kitchen drawer. Took me into a gentle hug and kiss. It was odd somehow. Threw me off the game. We were casual. We were friends with benefits. The benefits being the bigger part of the equation. I'm not sure we were friends. I had friends. I don't think he was on the list.

But there he was mucking around with my rolling pin. How had he gotten so comfortable at my apartment? Maybe it was because he'd been there three weeks out of the last four?

Usually, I'm the chatty one. I usually love to sit and talk for a few hours. But I didn't want that. All I wanted was the oblivion of sex. It's funny how much talk there is nowadays about "living in the moment" and "being in the present."

I'm finding that the only time I have those present moments are when I'm having sex. It's amazing how that can take my entire focus. Doesn't really give me time to think about anything or anyone else.

After Thunderbolt pulled a glass from my cabinet, poured himself a pale ale a friend had given him, and started to sit to chat, I did a slow blink.

"Look," I started. "I've had a really bad week. Like varsity level shitty."

"What happened?"

"I'm not the least bit interested in talking about it. My

week imploded somewhere between 'career suicide' and 'forensic accountant.'" I held up my hands for air quotes around the two big problems I'd had, ignoring the elephant in the living room of my mind.

I think my directness caught him off guard. He didn't even ask about Classic Car guy or mention that my apartment was surgery suite clean. I must have asked something because he was talking though I didn't hear a damned thing.

Somewhere in whatever he was saying he was talking how he'd chosen a college in upstate New York, going sight unseen, because that's where he'd learned about film and met the guy who'd made the beer, and, and...and I was thinking *right, sure, I don't care about any of that right now.*

Normally I loved talking to him and would have been interested in Rochester and beer and his friend. I had a deep and abiding love of other people's stories. Probably one of the things that made me love my job as an author. Fortunately, like most men, he was easily distracted.

If there were a contest for most enthusiastic and giving sex partner, Thunderbolt would win hands down. After I was quite satisfied and catching my breath, Thunderbolt was in my underwear drawer unearthing my box of Costco condoms. He picked a couple out, and put one on.

Then he came back to face me.

"You said that we could try it. Can we?"

"Try what?" It was an honest question. Eight orgasms in, I wasn't able to wade through the words he was saying to get to the meat of his question.

"Sex without a condom."

"Sure. If you want."

"I already opened this one," he said, talking after the close.

"Either way, that's a sunk cost."

Like a kid about to open a Christmas present, he stripped

off the condom. A long time later when he announced that he was at the end of his rope, he asked, "Can I come inside you?"

Honestly, I thought that was part of a package deal with no condom.

I shrugged, as much as one could during sex.

"Good, that's sweet of you."

And he did.

He dozed again. I didn't say a word until his eyes fluttered open. This time he didn't look at me like I was going to kill him in his sleep.

"I'm thinking of getting off dating apps," he announced.

"Why? I mean I disabled my profiles because I'm leaving for the summer. But why would you do it?"

"It makes me feel bad. It's like I'm commodifying women."

And he cared about that? I couldn't reconcile that with his happy ending massages, but even I was too tired to try to thread that needle. Plus I sort of loved that about Tinder. I was like Postmates for sex. Swipe, answer your door and there they are. It's how he'd ended up on my doorstep, bottle of Malbec in hand back in January.

"Do you think in this day and age you can meet a woman organically?" I wanted to cross my fingers in a hashtag, admit I was making fun of him from the week before, but I didn't.

"Maybe. I don't know. Maybe I'm not looking."

"Wow. Okay. I don't think I'm ready to do that quite yet."

"What are you looking for? Do you want a boyfriend?" he asked.

My mouth said, "I don't know." My brain screamed, yes, as a matter of fact I thought I had one until five days ago when I broke up with the one I may have had.

I didn't tell him about the list I'd written on a giant post it and affixed to the inside of my closet door at the advice of both a friend and my therapist. The list of what I wanted in a guy. What I wanted in a long -term relationship. What I wanted in, gasp—taboo word ahead—*a boyfriend*.

He yawned, big and long this time.

"When did you get back in town?" I asked.

"Yesterday. Saturday from Reno."

"When do you fly out again?"

"Tomorrow. Eight AM Vegas."

My smart watch glowed in the candlelight.

"It's nearly midnight."

"I've got to fly out of Burbank in the morning."

Burbank is not close to West Hollywood. There was really no freeway between the two, which made the twelve mile trip a long one by car in morning commute traffic.

"Geez. Louise. You need to get going."

"So when are you back?" he asked while hopping into his underwear. I'm not sure anyone looks dignified putting their underwear back on. Stripping is a one way street. He left the room scouring around the apartment for his clothes and anything else he'd dropped along the way. He appeared again fully dressed.

"August. End of August."

"So, I'll see you then."

"Um, sure." I didn't know what to do with that. Did he think oh, after the summer, we'd resume right where we left off? Wouldn't he be in some kind of serious relationship by then, his perfect woman having fallen from the sky, or off of romance authors who text too damn much and ask too many questions, but don't answer any?

He kissed me once sweetly, then again. It was the way I kissed Classic Car guy when I didn't want him to leave. Wrong kind of kiss from the wrong kind of person.

I let Thunderbolt out the door, leaving the outside light on only long enough so see him down my long walkway to the street where his rideshare car would soon be. Then I flipped it off and took myself to bed. My habit of texting too much hadn't waned. Thunderbolt was no exception to that. I'd rein it in one day. But today wasn't that day.

> **Me:** You made a bad, bad, shitty—did I mention it was bad?—week better. I'm going to find and friend you on FB so you can have more romance in your feed. Safe travels. G'night.

As I write this the next day, Monday, I'm still feeling just the tiniest bit unsettled.

Every moment I was with Classic Car guy, it was like I was holding on to smoke. I tried my hardest to try to be in the present moment with him. That living in the present thing that's all the rage in LA.

To try not to do anything that would make him up and skitter away. It didn't feel quite right, though. How was it I never found out where he lived more than vague generalities?

I mean I think I could pin it down to one of the cities in the San Gabriel valley, but that's the best I could do. Was it weird that he never scrubbed place info from the pictures he took all around the southland but those of his home couldn't be pinpointed by the best CIA agent? In the beginning I Googled, "is he having an affair?" Which of course led to "if you're googling this, you already know the answer."

That wasn't my hunch. My devout Christian friend said it was because he had less money and that maybe made him less than open. I'd told him I'd grown up poor. I'd shown him pictures from my family albums about my very humble beginnings. I thought he understood that one, I didn't judge based on money. Two, I wasn't a snob.

I also wondered why he went by his middle name. By the time I pretended to stumble on his first name, I'd already Googled that much. Or the fact that he refused to use a license plate. Weird. But people have their things, I'd rationalized. Or the fact that he mostly called me from his car.

One night we had a two -hour conversation while he was in his parked car. I've been in California for a long time. I might even love my car a little too much with its vanity plates that spell out the word 'author' surrounded by glittering rhinestones.

What I don't do ever is sit in it when it's not moving—well except on the freeway, but that couldn't be helped.

I still felt like there was some piece I wasn't seeing. Something that would give me a key to everything I felt like I didn't understand. But that's magical thinking. I could only make a decision based on the information I was given, which was sufficient to know I couldn't live with crumbs.

That had to be enough.

It was enough.

Or not enough.

Either way, I'd made an irreversible decision and had to live by it. In a way I felt like I was treating Thunderbolt like collateral damage. But Thunderbolt was a grown ass man who could at any time have nothing more to do with me. Who at least twice seemed to be heading that way before boomeranging back.

I'll insist to anyone who asks that Thunderbolt and I are not in a relationship. But we are. Not boyfriend and girlfriend, that's for sure. But lovers, I guess. Maybe even friends.

TWENTY-EIGHT

Summertime

JUNE 14.

A COUPLE of plane rides later, and I'm was in my summer house. Every year for the last seven, I've looked forward to summer more than anyone who hates the heat has a right to. But when I was on one of my twice -a -year crisis calls with my therapist right after announcing I was leaving my marriage, I had a harsh realization.

"At least you have your summer house to look forward to," she'd said. "You'll be leaving in a few days. That's always been a delight in your life."

"It's not the same when I don't have anything to run away from," I'd said.

The delight, I think, in going away for an entire summer was that I was escaping the abusive husband. Two and a half months of not being berated, yelled at, screamed at, pretend pushed or punched. Who wouldn't want to escape all that for the peace and quiet of somewhere else—*anywhere* else.

I was reading a journal entry from a year ago June. I could not wait to get on a plane, I'd said, away from the man who treats me as a receptacle for his anger and semen.

He's still angry. I bear the brunt of that more times a day

than I can count with endless messages and manipulation of my child. But it's, for the most part, at a distance of ten miles, which in L.A. might as well be ninety. So I'm left with just me facing an uncertain future and a summer outside of Southern California.

A few weeks ago Thunderbolt asked me if I was planning on taking a lover for the summer. I shrugged, because I'd thought about it in passing but not too deeply. Not when I'd been embroiled in trying to make my relationship with Classic Car guy something it was not.

"What are the men like there?" he'd asked of my summer home outside the U.S.

"Kind of macho," I said. West Hollywood and Los Angeles for that matter were full of men bent on being feminist and sympathetic and kind. Not saying they achieved it at all if Me Too revelations were any indication. But they seem to start out with those intentions outwardly. Outside of Southern California and probably the West Coast, things were different.

I'd poked around on Tinder a few months back when I was there in the spring and I was startled by what I'd seen. Men who all listed their education. Who looked like they'd decided to give up on their appearance post forty. I mean I get it. LA's Tinder is full of carefully airbrushed headshots. So outside of southern California I knew things would be different. They were startling nonetheless.

I was thinking of changing my profile to say, "looking for a summer fling," or something similar.

I logged on to Tinder the first or second night after I'd landed. It was overwhelming. I felt like I had my freshman year of college when the upper class guys referred to us as fresh meat and swarmed us like sharks on chum.

It seemed like everyone I swiped right on was a match. I even considered the offer of a cute guy, but chickened out at the last minute when he went from sexy to creepy.

The memory of the nearly gymnastic sex with Thunderbolt was still fresh in my mind and it was enough in the face of lots of new faces.

I swiped occasionally and held a few conversations, but my heart wasn't in it. Three weeks later, it was a different story.

TWENTY-NINE

The Sociologist

JULY.

I'D BEEN ONLY OCCASIONALLY MESSAGING various guys until I matched with The Sociologist. He was thirty -two and was a dead ringer for Peter MacNicol if Peter MacNicol was thirty -two. Think Ally McBeal MacNicol not Veep MacNicol. A sociologist by profession, he was in the middle of pursuing his Ph.D. I can't say why he stood out, but he did.

The conversation on Tinder started like many of them did, I think.

> **The Sociologist:** Heyho, luckily I love kissing :) And I'll be back in town on Monday. Till when are you staying?
> **Me:** I live here half the year. Here next week then trav-eling to a few cities before I come back home.
> **The Sociologist:** Oh, cool :) And what brought you to town? I'm arriving Monday quite late, would you be up for meeting around 10 PM?
> **The Sociologist:** By the way, how about adding each other on Facebook?

That was my first Facebook invitation. Classic Car claimed not to use Facebook, but he had an account. It was, of course, a picture of his car. Which he'd texted to me. Which is how I knew it was him even though he used a different name on Tinder.

Friending Thunderbolt had been a huge deal for him. Like somehow I was going to openly acknowledge him on that platform. I'd never do it because I had a lot more to lose than he did with a jealous and erratic ex, but I didn't tell him that.

This connection was so open and honest, he probably hooked me in with that. Oh and being cute, of course. Really cute in only the way a man in his early thirties can be.

Me: I have an early morning breakfast so 10 is too late. Time for coffee or a drink another day?

July 17.

The Sociologist: Added you. Also your site seems cool :) I guess we'll need to meet next week then, but a drink would be lovely.

You know what I have a weakness for? The word lovely. Thunderbolt used it and so did this guy. It's a delightful word that warms my heart. It's the magic key to getting into my pants.

After that, he stopped messaging me on Tinder. Moved to Facebook.

The Sociologist: Heyy.

Men are so original like that. I so often wonder what happens in their brains. I can't believe we let them run countries.

Me: Hey there. (Irony completely lost on him) Traveling today?
The Sociologist: Heyho, yepp. I'm a bit sad we can't meet today, you seem so cool and interesting, and also very cute. :)

I never know what to say to this. Not the first time. Not the fiftieth. I had almost zero control over my looks. That? That was genetics. I do the best with what I have, but it's not what defines me.

Me: Thanks. Just got back from breakfast. Meals are loooong here and I have to work as I like to keep a roof over my head. How's your week looking??
The Sociologist: Well, right now I'm out of town and should get working as my connection flight only leaves in the evening. Tomorrow I'll go to my workplace and then to a festival. How about you? What are you working on?

Monday 3:58 PM

Me: I'm a writer so writing. I'm working on the last book in a trilogy. It's a romance where it takes the couple twenty plus years to finally get together. It's one of my favorite ones. Which festival? I'll be at a medieval one this weekend. What do you do for work?
The Sociologist: Ooh, nice. And do you take inspirations from your life? What kind of connections are you looking for? I'll be at a music festival at the lake. Would you like to visit me? I'm a sociologist.

That first question was the one I hated the most. I know it was inspired by my occupation listing on my profile. And I'd done just that to get the creepy questions out of the way. The two people who didn't ask—upfront at least—were Classic Car and Thunderbolt.

They surely asked later, but not at first. It's kind of exhausting. If I wrote books, say about serial killers, I doubted I'd get the same question. The irony of all this was that readers often said they loved my sex scenes. I'd had so little sex in my real life before my divorce, I'm sure they'd be surprised that it was all imagination. Probably my most inspired work.

Me: I haven't been to the lake in a couple of years. Zero inspiration from life. Ah, the what are you looking for question.

And here I was straight up honest.

Me: I thought I knew the answer to that last month or last year. Now, who knows? I'm mostly interested in meeting and getting to know new people and seeing where it goes—which is probably a very wishy washy answer.

The Sociologist: I don't think there is anything wrong with this answer. What happened last month? Anyways, I was asking because you should know that I'm in an open relationship, so I'm looking for friends and maybe sensual connections, definitely not one - night stand, but also not a super serious relationship.

I didn't answer about what happened last month. I was thrilled to not be crying about Classic Car Guy most days. Still dreamed about him a lot of nights, but the days were something I'd gotten a handle on.

The only thoughts were fond ones of someone who seemed to genuinely like me—which I'd rarely experienced—and post mortems on why I'd ignored the fact that he stood me up about half the time. Was it a lack of self -esteem or fear of confrontation? I was still working out that puzzle most days. I got off line and got back to the business of writing and parenting.

The Sociologist: (three hours later) hope i didn't scare you away.
Me: No. Just busy working. Not scared. I was on the bus when I was messaging before...
The Sociologist: oki, then i'll wait for your answer 🩶
Me: I have dinner in a bit...but I'm open to something casual.
The Sociologist: perfect, that's what i'm looking for too, something longer term based on friendship, but no expectations whatsoever, just pure fun
Me: I think we're very much on the same page...

In my head was a ringing sound because I think he'd mastered the message game. He was up for something casual, but not a one off. Clearly, I'm not opposed to a one off, but that's honestly a bit of work I didn't want to have to repeat time and again while I was out of West Hollywood for the summer. A regular guy was something that Thunderbolt had come to make me appreciate.

Go him.

The Sociologist: :)) Can't wait to meet. How do you usually have free time?

The one thing about summer is that I have my kid full

time, no respite. Very occasionally I have a babysitter, but ninety-nine percent of the time, he's with me. This means that I do all my socializing, museum visits, and work during the eight hours he's at day camp. That worked when I was married. Even though the marriage was a disaster, I never cheated.

So there was no way I could do what I did in L.A., and step out late at night for a drink. Nor could I invite anyone over.

But I was willing to meet for coffee or a drink and if it was promising, I could make arrangements.

Once the Sociologist understood these limitations, he did something surprising.

Accommodated them.

He was away for the weekend in a nearby town at the lake for four days with friends. I was quite surprised when he said he'd be willing to come back so we could meet.

I really had to sit with it for a good twelve hours.

Getting Classic Car Guy to meet me when we were both free and only a few miles apart was like an act of Congress. Obviously, as the last two times he stood me up brought me to my breaking point, or breaking up point.

And this guy, whom I'd never met in person, who did not profess to like me, adore me, want to be with me, was willing to take a break from time with his friends and drive back to meet me. All he wanted in return was a commitment that I'd meet him if he made that effort.

I was willing to travel a half mile if he traveled thirty. So a two o'clock meeting was proposed. I accepted.

The Sociologist: Let's meet at the park. We can just walk around, or if there is chemistry, we can walk towards my place. 😃

There was no equivocation in that. If I was game, I was going to get laid.

For all the dates I'd been on, I hadn't been nervous— except with Classic Car and Thunderbolt—maybe because I liked them the best. Before I left my house, I was nervous.

Get up from the computer and get out the vacuum nervous.

Take a second shower nervous.

Consider then abandon the idea of polishing my toenails nervous.

But he'd already come thirty miles from the festival grounds, so I had to get off my butt and make the trip even though there was a strong urge to stay home and hide behind the glow of the laptop screen.

I usually love my body more days than not. But for some reason this last week there hasn't been much love. It was inching up on half past the hour and I wasn't going to get any thinner or any prettier in the next five minutes.

I set out at one -thirty and made the walk to the bus. We were going to meet in a local park. That was a first.

Like always I was there early. I took a seat on a bench about fifty feet from where we were supposed to meet and picked up the Kindle to calm me down. Unfortunately, the pigeons thought I was there to give them treats (damn you people who feed these flying rats) and swarmed around me. I put the ereader away, took out my phone and messaged him. A guy had to be better than pigeons any day.

Me: I'm here, what are you wearing?
The Sociologist: Blue shirt. I'm at the meeting spot.
Me: I'm on a bench being heckled by pigeons.
The Sociologist: Hmmm.

He was exactly who he said he was. His pictures were definitely an accurate representation of who he was. Probably the most honest guy I'd met on Tinder.

Thunderbolt's pictures were at least two years old as were Classic Car Guy's. They'd won me over because they were both good with words and still cute in person, if a bit older.

There wasn't a single thing about this guy that didn't work for me. So I did something I'd never done. When the Sociologist asked, "So do you want to go somewhere or back to my place?"

I said, "Your place."

One of my rules had been never to go to a guy's place. Not the first time we met. But I was in my summer place and felt all the more trusting for that. I couldn't say why, but I did. Although maybe it was because it had a murder rate that was like a thousandth of Southern California's, or because guns were mostly illegal.

"I live just over there," he said pointing toward the river.

"How did you end up there?" I asked.

"Inherited the place from my grandparents," he acknowledged. "I have to apologize, though. It's messy. I've been traveling so much I haven't had a chance to clean."

Flashed right back to visiting Thunderbolt's place for the first—and only—time. Since it's been pretty much established that my house is fairly neat, I have no idea how to interpret other people's messes.

I couldn't even wrap my head around what level of mess would make me turn tail and run. We walked the few blocks to his place, and I held my breath.

He stuck the keys in the lock, and I followed him in. It was both better and worse than I expected. It was the oddest combination. A bachelor pad layered on top of old people stuff.

"Coffee, tea, wine, beer?"

I checked my watch. It was two -thirty. I took the wine,

happy that I'd take the bus to pick up my kid and I didn't drive at all during the summers. So day wine was okay.

It was a crisp Greek wine. He cleared a bunch of travel receipts from his couch and I took a seat. He sat close enough to touch and we talked about travel mostly. He'd been away, I was going away, and we compared notes.

Halfway through my wine, he put his hand on my denim-clad thigh and looked at me.

"Can I kiss you?"

For a moment, it was a total throwback to high school when I dated a boy who asked me that. I nodded, and he leaned in. I realized then that if I were in charge of these damned dates, they'd never go anywhere.

Drummer Boy made the first move. Classic Car Guy did as well. Thunderbolt had his memorable, 'break the ice line," and Justin Time took charge.

The kiss wasn't perfect. Wasn't going to set the world on fire. But it was good enough. Then he leaned in closer and kissed me on the neck. When my ex had done that, I'd hated it. Always worried he was going to somehow strangle me.

The feeling here was the exact opposite. It felt amazing. It also made me just a little bit uncomfortable because it was such an intimate act.

When he sat back to take a breath, I held up the goblet of white wine in my hand.

"Let me put this down," I said. "I had a red wine accident last month and I don't care to repeat it."

I took a big sip of the wine, then set it on the table.

"Do you want to go into the bedroom?" he asked.

That was it. The reason I'd been on Tinder. The likely reason he'd been on Tinder.

"Sure." I stood and followed him through the door to the large room that held his bed as well as a computer and other work stuff. For a moment we talked about his ergonomic chair, then I took a seat on his covers, white with huge green leaves.

The Sociologist stretched out, I lay down, and he kissed me in earnest. I closed my eyes and enjoyed it. My shirt was first to go, then his. I could feel his hand against the smooth back of my bra and almost laughed at what I knew would be a perplexed face if I could see it.

"How do you..."

I sat up, took the front clasp in hand and made the magic happen. Then he really made the magic. For some reason I thought that sex outside of L.A. would be vastly different. But it wasn't. It was very much the same and he was very good. I came twice before he even took off his pants. Once I recovered, I gestured toward his khaki shorts...

A week or two before this, I was listening to one of the sex podcasts and one of the guests was saying that every time you met a new man, you never knew what you'd find when you opened his pants. It was a little—she said—like unwrapping a gift and not knowing what you were getting. For me, it was like choosing a door on Let's Make a Deal.

What kind of penis am I going to get today?

Before his orange boxer briefs came off, there was one thing I was pretty sure of. His penis would be uncut. The place where I summered is known for keeping boys uncircumcised.

Before Classic Car Guy, I'd never seen one on an adult man before. I was ninety-nine percent sure that's what was coming out. I wasn't disappointed...about that. I put my hand around it and it was the smallest I'd ever felt. Despite my inability to keep most things to myself, I didn't comment on that. Once I jerked him once or twice, he wasn't thinking much about anything I had to say, no doubt.

I was working on how to deal with the condom issue. Mine were in my purse by the front door. I had no idea what he had or where it might be when he came all over my leg. That problem was solved in an instant.

I took myself to the bathroom to wash up. He wanted to cuddle when I came back. I did for as long as I could be still... which for me wasn't very long, then I sat up and started putting on my clothes.

"My girlfriend and I have an open arrangement because she's out of town for the next four months," he volunteered.

"I get it," I said. "My regular guy asked me if I was going to take a lover over the summer."

"What's he like?"

Before I could think better of it, I answered.

"We're friends on Facebook. He's a filmmaker." Then I proceeded to tell him about the damned movie that Thunderbolt had on the circuit. Sometimes my mouth does not keep up with my brain on using discretion.

"Can we do this again? Monday?" he asked when I was done singing Thunderbolt's praises.

"Maybe. Probably," I said. "But with travel, I'm not sure. I might have some last minute errands."

"Let me know," he said as he watched me try to fasten my front clasping bra for the umpteenth time.

"Damned thing," I swore.

"You should leave it," he said. "It's sexy as hell."

"Maybe," I said. "But I certainly can't get on the bus like this."

His smile was slow, knowing. "No. Probably not."

I waited a good seven hours before I texted him.

Fed the kid.

Did the bath routine.

Cooked the dinner.

Washed the dishes.

I don't know what the urge is I have to reach out. But clearly I hadn't overcome it. I messaged: Thanks for a delightful afternoon. I hope you got a good nap in. Have a good festival weekend. Let's talk. Maybe we can get together early next week...

The Sociologist: Yess, it was really lovely to meet. Hope we'll see each next Monday.

Then I didn't see him again for two weeks. I took my kid on a trip. Then I went on a solo trip myself.

THIRTY

The Micropenis

JULY 28.

AFTER I WASHED what seemed like a thousand loads of laundry from our impromptu vacation to the mountains, I messaged the Sociologist. My son was with his father for the second half of the summer, and outside of writing, I had a lot of time on my hands.

A lot.

Maybe too much.

Me: Flying back now. You have some time this weekend?

The Sociologist: heyho, most probably the weekend won't work, but do you maybe have some time during the week?

Me: Absolutely. My schedule is quite clear now.

The Sociologist: awesome 😊 maybe Tuesday or Wednesday afternoon then?

By Saturday though, I was happy to say that he'd moved us up to Monday.

The Sociologist: could perhaps Monday work, around 3-4pm? perfect :)) i'll try to arrive between 3 and 4, but i'll keep you posted. can't wait to be with you again :))

Like Thunderbolt, he was timely. I'd kind of forgotten how cute he was or how sexy his accent was.

We talked a little about his job and the project he was working on (a study of people's attitudes toward self-driving cars and other AI in the transportation realm). I gave him a tour of my summer place. (What was up with FWB being fascinated with how I lived?) I swear this is another two-bedroom like mine in West Hollywood. But he liked my color choice. Let me say he got bonus points for NOT pointing out that it was neat, though I could totally see it was on the tip of his tongue. The 'N' word that he expressed was 'nice.' To paint a scene: it's basically all Ikea, with artwork I've collected.

I promise you, dear reader, that I'm not a neat freak or a fabulous decorator. Single men are just weird.

We skipped day drinking this time and got comfortable on my couch. This couch is not as legendary as the West Hollywood one, but it's...white. Yes, getting a white couch with a son was not my best idea, but it's a summer house and I wanted something...summery. Most days I don't regret it. But I refused to make out on it. Accidents could happen.

So we moved to my bedroom. My ex has refused to get his stuff out of our summer house. I have finally packed most of it up, but it's not all gone. For a few long minutes that Monday morning I wondered if it would be weird to sleep in the same bed I'd slept in with my ex. (Granted, my ex had only come down a couple of weeks a year. I mostly slept here alone.) Or if would be weird that my ex's shoes were still in the closet.

Turned out the minute the Sociologist came through the door I wasn't thinking jack shit about my ex. The thing I like the most about this guy is that he's pretty giving. My guess is that it has to do with the size of his package.

So one night having finished my word count for the day, I did a deep dive on penis size and whether or not his was what some people call a micro penis.

Now look, I have some thoughts on the penises I've encountered in my life, but suffice it to say they've all more or less done the job—except my ex—but for that one I'm honestly very grateful. The less of that, the better. Anyway, I've spent more time thinking about his penis than anyone should. I think it would qualify as a micro. There was a lot of differing advice on what to do when women encountered one. Lots of advice for men on what the owners of a very small penis should do to 'make up' for it.

At the end of the day, the Sociologist was giving enough that I was willing to forgo all the deep thrusting I liked. Not everyone can be everything.

THIRTY-ONE

The Surrendered Single

AUGUST 4.

BASED on the advice of these dating books and podcasts, I updated my online profile pic on Tinder, OkCupid, and Bumble to be a smiling picture...

It was dead serious shot before—which *I* thought was sexier.

So I wake up to a notification on Tinder...and you guessed it. Classic Car guy has also updated his pic...eight hours later. Eight hours and seven months later, I should add. He hadn't updated it after I met him. Don't ask me how I know that.

I *know* I should unmatch... Let's just say that I'm proud I didn't click the green heart next to the pictures OR message him. See...I have restraint.

In answer to your question: Yes, he looks hawt in the picture. Yes I'm super judgey about the fact that he posted pictures where he's wearing what we Americans affectionately call a wife beater— a white tank top.

NO he didn't update his profile from "no drama, no issues" to "heaps and buckets of drama and I *will* stand you up..." Though he has been married three times, so maybe I'm the only person who's been stood up.

201

THIRTY-TWO

The HIV Test

AUGUST 14.

THE BEST PART of listening to podcasts on dating is I've learned a ton. A year ago a friend sent me a box of books on dating. I stacked them on a bookcase unread and immediately moved on to downloading dating apps. I'm not in West Hollywood so I can't say if the books are any good.

What have been informative and probably life changing are the podcasts. All the hand wringing and brain space I've wasted on dating could have been saved if I'd known just a bit of the knowledge from the first ten hours I listened to the first thing in the morning the last couple of weeks.

Have you heard of breadcrumbing or e-tethering?

Nope?

Me either until last week.

Apparently that's what Classic Car guy did. It's a thing, his particular pathology. Guy comes on strong, says wonderful things to you. Strokes your ego. Has sex with you early in the relationship.

Disappears.

Then reappears.

Then disappears.

But can't make plans. It has a name, or many names starting with emotional unavailability and ending with e-tethering.

Guys do it to keep you on the hook, maybe while they're doing it to someone else, maybe not. Who knows? I can't believe I didn't Google this before. If I'd known the term, I'd have saved myself hours of worrying.

The second lesson. There's nothing to be won by being the "cool girl," the girl who doesn't want to be too needy. Have too much drama. Require any kind of respectful treatment. Apparently, there's nothing to be gained from being the cool girl. Except guys who won't respect your time. Won't respect you.

So I'm done being the cool girl.

I might miss her a little bit, though.

This revelation came on the heels of the worst case of hives I've ever had. My first few weeks of the summer I had a swollen lymph node that wouldn't go away. Then the allergic reaction. Started as a small rash then turned into hives everywhere. Itchy bumpy hives.

Google is not your friend. I spent too much time in between writing chapters Googling lymph nodes and hives. Those were two of the nine thousand symptoms of HIV. That's when I started worrying. In my "cool girl" mode, I'd been sporadic with condoms with Classic Car Guy. Plus the single time with Thunderbolt, though I believed him when he said he was clean. God knows I know better, but I did it anyway.

Because, you know, cool girls with little self -respect and less self -esteem roll like that.

While I was in between doctor's appointments where all the medical professionals seem stumped by my hives, I Googled anonymous HIV testing. I ran to the doctor after the first time I slept with Classic Car guy because I never suspected I'd repeat the mistake. All my tests came back clean.

But that was only a week or two after the exposure. After discovering that the virus isn't active until one or two months after exposure. I realized that I hadn't waited long enough.

So I took my Google fu and used it to find an anonymous and free testing center on the other side of town. Took the bus for forty -five minutes and got in line.

You can only the imagine the instant camaraderie of standing in a line of people who are getting anonymous STD testing. We bonded, we waited. I got tested. They have a fast test. They prick your finger, put your blood on a stick and like a pregnancy test, it gives you results in twenty minutes.

I made a promise to myself on the ride over to the testing office. If I was negative, I'd immediately unmatch from Classic Car Guy on Tinder and I'd delete him from my phone.

I pulled a number at the center as soon as it opened. I was A82—number five in line. I watched a really handsome guy with piercing blue eyes go in first. He didn't look happy. Then two teenage girls who were up way too early for the amount of mascara they were sporting, went next. Then the technician called A81. He was long gone.

"Happens all the time," the technician said. He pointed at me and my little number slip. "You're next."

He gave an explanation of the anonymous nature of the test. Asked me where I was born and my year of birth—for statistical purposes. Also to give me a nickname.

Then I went back into a second room where a very cheerful guy with socks and sandals asked me about my job. I told him I wrote romance. Then he pricked my finger, took blood, and put it on a test strip. Gave me a note with my time to return and the next person went in.

During that twenty -minute wait, I tried to show myself compassion. But there was a bit of self -flagellation thrown in. How could I have been so cavalier about my health when I have a nine -year -old child who will need me at *least* another nine years if not a whole lot more.?

While I was waiting, my phone pinged. My summer FWB, The Sociologist, said he'd like to come by that afternoon. Normally that would have made me smile. But hives combined with sitting in a free clinic was anything but a turn on. I didn't respond and crossed my fingers hoping he was too busy with work.

Twenty minutes later, they called the first three people in. They didn't seem devastated, so I'm guessing they were negative. I wanted to continue that streak. The clinician called me over to look at the test. The control line was there, but the positive line wasn't.

I'd dodged the hell of a bullet with some dignity, self-esteem, and self-regard intact.

I'm not one hundred percent sure what that will mean when I get back to West Hollywood, but it for sure won't look like the past few months.

THIRTY-THREE

Damnit, You Can't Go Back

SEPTEMBER 2.

A SUMMER away reinforced Classic Car Guy's emotional unavailability. But I knew it was the same for Thunderbolt even though I think I didn't want it to be true. So I made a pact with myself: I would not under any circumstances reach out to him.

If he never called again, I'd brush off my hands and move on. I hadn't been home from my summer vacation for more than a handful of days before he texted.

Thunderbolt: Back in town?
Me: I am. Are you?
Thunderbolt: Indeed.

The vibe we had going before was that after this, I'd cut to the chase and invite him over. Then he'd drag out some kind of reluctant response. It was emotionally exhausting to feel like I was on the chase. Plus I was busy, so I didn't respond at all. Thirty minutes later I get another text.

Thunderbolt: Busy later?

Me: Tonight. Yes. Have kid. Tomorrow is free.

Then I reached out on Labor Day because it was my only child free day out of a dozen. And I wanted to see him. And I wanted to get laid.

That text set off a series of fantasies in my mind. In them he was super cool and interested in my life. How we'd pick up on all the funny and interesting threads we'd dropped when I left. How there would be all this amazing sex.

Trust me when I say that I knew I was spinning out fantasies in my head. What I couldn't put my finger on was what in the hell was really going to be.

All that chemistry from June? It had fizzled out when he showed up on my doorstep on a hot as heck night in September. I'm not sure what I wanted or expected, but it was all a paler shade of what had been.

We chatted. We kissed. We did the acrobatic sex thing and it was all just meh. It was as if all his emotional unavailability made him less attractive.

It went from eight orgasms a night in June—eight!—to none in September. No matter what he did, I couldn't...I didn't feel anything.

What do I do with that? I've been following the Michael Steinberg method and had worked up one very interesting conversation with a guy. Another had started off promising before it devolved into a conversation about his boot fetish.

Pro tip: getting your fetish out front—good. Not getting to know a person before getting your fetish out there—bad. Another cute guy was just too damned young. He was the same age as Classic Car Guy, and maybe almost as immature.

Nine months in. Nine months of dating, and I feel like I'm back at square one.

On Thursday I was lying in bed, waiting for sleep to come when I realized I missed a big social cue. I'm not sure how much therapy I'm going to need, but I'd do anything to fix not only my guy picker but my cue reader.

Did I mention that Thunderbolt got all dressed up? It only took me three days to notice that he'd made that kind of effort. Then immediately I felt bad because I'd been a bit of an asshole.

If dating was a mirror, mine wasn't showing a very kind reflection. After a half hour of debate, I decided to send a text.

Me: It was good seeing you Monday night.

Before I sent that, I did the thing all the mindfulness books tell you to do. Divorce yourself from the outcome. I decided I'd send a message to be nice where I maybe hadn't been in person. He'd put himself out there and I'd spun around in my head. After I hit send, I went to sleep. I woke up to.

Thunderbolt: Same here.

There's nothing to do with that, but leave it there. I packed my weekend with a dating and relationship seminar, theater and drinks with mom friends. If he texted, then of course I'd say yes, otherwise, I'd let it ride.

THIRTY-FOUR

The One Where I Learn Nothing

CHANGING the brain wiring of adults is a difficult thing. All I'm reading about brain science suggests it takes a very concerted effort. Because I'm nothing if not up for a challenge, I'm trying it anyway.

First, there's an online class, often referred to as The Happiness Class, that I'm taking. Turns out what humans think will make them happy doesn't. Also I've discovered that humans misread each other much of the time. The stories we tell ourselves about other people and our relationships with them are just that—stories.

My soon-to-be rewired brain made a couple of decisions in the last few weeks.

First, I'd decided that I was going to stop messing with Thunderbolt. That catnip of push -pull isn't healthy for anyone. Second, I'm was going to not only expand the pool of people I'm willing to date, I'm was going to be myself.

One hundred percent myself. God save these men from all of me.

I'm shelving "cool girl," and "funny girl," and "drinky girl."

All my personas are going to be shoved deep into storage at the back of my virtual closet.

The conversation I had with a trusted mentor led me straight to that last decision. I was going on about how I didn't know how to act like a normal, securely attached person on a date. Every man I'd had a relationship with had told me in no uncertain terms that I was "too much."

Too loud.

Too talkative.

To opinionated.

Too much bling.

You name it, it's all been too much for someone. So I asked her if I should continue to "tone myself down."

To me, she replied, "You know how you've described your son as a big personality?"

"Of course," I said. Long story short, my son is bold, brash, outgoing, extraverted, and quite chatty. He's a lot of fun, but I can see that, when others really talk and listen to him, he can seem like a handful because he's like the sun. You turn your face to it because it's warm, but you can't stare at it, because it's big and bright and full on.

"Would you ever tell your son to act differently for anyone?"

"No! Of course not!" My answer couldn't have been more emphatic. Then I paused as she gave me one of those looks that said I needed to make a leap in my mind.

"Oh," I finally said.

She nodded. "Just be you. Someone will love all of you just as you are."

That's the person I took out on a Thursday night date to Culver City. Following the lead of all the dating books I've been reading, I let the guy plan the date. Up until now, not one of them had planned anything. This is how I ended up at an

Italian restaurant across the street from The Ripped Bodice (the only all romance bookstore in the L.A. area).

I've been debating on a nickname for this one, but let's call him The Hiker. It took two weeks or more maybe to set up a date because he'd been heavily pursuing his new hobby—hiking. And not the kind of hiking I do, up a sandy hill in L.A. and back down again in an hour. His hiking took him to Yosemite's Half Dome last week and Mount Baldy the week before. Nope, I don't know where Mount Baldy is, and I'm not finding out.

I connected with the Hiker on OkCupid. That whole thing about swiping right on all the people who had above a ninety something percent match percentage one dating expert suggested? I did that. He was at ninety-two.

The thing about expanding age ranges, I did that.

He's fifty seven.

Also my new personal criteria was someone who had traveled. I love to travel and sharing that with someone with a passport and familiarity with lots of different countries was important to me. The Hiker is a native of a small town in Denmark. Before landing in L.A., he'd been all over the world.

The Hiker lives in Playa del Rey, which is one of those small communities that's both desirable and undesirable in equal measure. It's near the airport and also near the ocean.

So I agreed that Culver City was a happy medium between him and West Hollywood. He did offer to come my way, but I was tired of all the places near me. Also, I didn't want to run into anyone I knew in WeHo. Except for romance authors at whatever event the bookstore was hosting, the likelihood of meeting anyone I knew while dining in Culver City was close to a zero probability.

I don't want to say the date was boring. Because it wasn't. It was just...uneventful. He did not spend any time trying to seduce me like Classic Car Guy had done quite successfully. He didn't spend hours complimenting me or talking about how sexy I was (too many guys to count).

It was a tell me about you kind of date. I talked about writing and traveling. He talked about his job (logistics) and his new passion for hiking. It was two -and -a -half hours and I wish I could say more.

It was...pleasant.

He wasn't bat shit crazy or wildly inappropriate, which seem to be my two favorite flavors.

I'd probably have talked longer, but the restaurant closed the kitchen early, and I had to get back home because I had a painter coming first thing in the morning. Sleep seemed important...until it didn't. While I was driving, Apple Car Play was happy to have Siri read this message:

The Hiker: Jolie, thanks for a lovely time and conversation. Be safe and I look forward to speaking with you again soon. The Hiker 'He signed his real name like it was a letter.' That, people, is what fifty-seven got you.

Instead of responding by voice while I was driving home, I decided to meditate on it. Think about what the real me would say. The dating advice books I've binged and podcasts that have dominated my Bluetooth speakers have focused on one thing.

Saying yes.

If he's not crazy, go on that second date. One date isn't enough to know anything, they say. It was enough for me to know one thing, I was on the fence about dating someone significantly older. The Hiker appeared to be young at heart, fit and in shape—as one has to be to do eight hours of hiking over 4000 feet of elevation. But he was old in other ways. In my head I'd pegged him firmly at sixty.

There were wrinkles in the part of his body that I could see. Liver spots are a real thing. My head spun out to what it would be like to see him naked. Would it be attractive? Could he get it up? Would he be able to keep it up? Up until now, the oldest penises I'd seen had belonged to my ex and Drummer Boy, neither of whom could maintain an erection. That was too much for my brain to hold in, so I tabled it.

If you know anything about Thunderbolt's timing, you know that the minute I was done with the date, when I was thinking how a sane secure person with high self-esteem would respond to the Hiker's text, Thunderbolt was right there blowing up my phone.

Thunderbolt: Hi.
Me: Hey.

I know, I know. Hay is for horses. But I was tired of trying to read a whole bunch of bullshit into his two letter texts. I was tired of feeling like I was begging for his company. So I'd decided I wasn't doing it anymore.

Thunderbolt: Up and about?
Me: Kind of. Long day.

It had been a long day of kid stuff, breakfast with a friend who moved back to L.A., an appointment with an allergist, and thinking about being my true self on a date. That and driving all around the city had taken it out of me.

Thunderbolt: Save it for another?
Me: Ever get that feeling that English is not your first language...
Thunderbolt: Ha.
Me: I'm lost.
Thunderbolt: Aw, I think that's just your process and many artist's process. Total self -doubt before the turn-around and inevitable finish.

Me: Are you fucking with me? I didn't even drink tonight.
Thunderbolt: Not fucking with you. What?
Me: I didn't understand the 'save it for another' text then I lost the plot.
Thunderbolt: Ha. I meant should I come over and fool around or save it for another night? Because you sounded tired.
Me: Got it. Jeez. That was hard.
Thunderbolt: Ha.
Me: How long is Ad Astra?
Thunderbolt: Two hours
Me: My adult self the one who's having a painter come at the ass crack of dawn has to say another day. The adult self who loves sex is not happy...
Thunderbolt: Ha
Me: Other than Ad Astra (I have to go) I'm free tomorrow.
Thunderbolt: I'm in Denver tomorrow but back Monday.

Did you see that boss move? Nothing like the creation of scarcity and FOMO to wake someone up.

Me: Well now... I'm caring less about getting up early
Me: and now that I've changed my mind, he's off the phone...
Thunderbolt: Haha I'm down. Sorry was emailing assistant
Me: Adulting is good.
Thunderbolt: Indeed.
Me: LMK
Thunderbolt: K I'm gonna take a real quick shower

and come by. I usually Uber but is there parking at your place?

Me: Yes. I have a 2d space.

Thunderbolt: Ok so pull in the back and it's there. Me: Yes. Next to the blue SUV. The driveway is on the right.

Thunderbolt has never driven to my house. Because West Hollywood is horrible to park in at night, and his older building had no designated parking, he never risked losing his space and instead opted for the five dollar Uber ride around the corner.

Instead of the walking up my front walk, I heard the sound of a motor pulling behind my place. I poked my head out to make sure he found the back stairs.

Why he drove? I couldn't say then because he didn't preview the most important part of all that driving until much later.

All I can report is that he bought himself a luxury convertible. I'd test driven the car the year it came out because my ex wanted it. Ultimately, he bought a more luxurious car, but I remember the ride.

Before I lose the plot here, back to Thunderbolt. He was his delightful lovely self, not his shitty asshole self. He was about to embark on three or four weeks of travel around the U.S. showing his film. He was also happy that he'd had three or four offers for distribution.

I know that the push-pull is catnip for the maladjusted. I'm not unaware, but there I was with him on my tie-dye sheets anyway. A few weeks ago, I thought you couldn't go back. I couldn't have been more wrong. We were back in a groove. Probably the best sex I'd had this year, hands down.

A friend once asked me what I like about him. I said to her he "tried hard." I think that sounds negative, but really it's not.

Rather than just going about it like it's a chore, he was really an enthusiastic partner.

So, like the Mafia I was back in, even if just a little bit. The Hiker, out of my mind, just like that. I did get up the next morning and thank him for the date. But like a true avoidant I dithered over sending something, and until I sat down to write this, didn't think or worry one second about his response.

THIRTY-FIVE

The Married Man

SEPTEMBER 24.

IT HAD TO HAPPEN.

The odds of meeting only single and available people online are not one hundred percent.

Enter: The Married Man.

To be one hundred percent clear, when I came back to California after a summer away, I'd changed my profile from 'I don't know' or some derivation to 'Long-term Relationship,' or the equivalent on the various apps.

In my head that implied that the man had to be available for that. Men must have some completely different understanding of the English language. It's like the match I got yesterday from a guy where our OkCupid compatibility was at ninety-six percent. He was good looking and I was happily clicking through his profile until he got to the description of the woman he wanted: she had to be thin.

I looked down at my post baby body, a full-length picture of which I'd included in my profile following dating expert advice. Because men are visual, if they don't like how you look, they'll "swipe left" and move on.

So I included a shot from the summer where I'm wearing a short skirt and short sleeves. My profile reads: curvy, and yet this guy clicked on me. For a hot minute, I considered swiping right because except for that one caveat it looked like we'd have gotten on like a house on fire. This paragraph long digression was just a quick illustration of the fact that men don't read.

I'm going to be honest, the first text from the Married Man off app wasn't a surprise. His screen name was Vic, but he messaged with his real name. I'd learned from Drummer Boy that a lot of people don't use their real name. Some obvious like: JackedGuy or SexyGuy, but others weren't obvious because they were real names, just not the *guy's* real name.

After his real name, his opening salvo was a picture of him on vacation with his adult children. It was a great shot. He sent some others of him at the Hollywood Bowl, an open air live music venue, at the Pantages Theater in Hollywood and him traveling abroad this year.

As I love live performance and travel, I was kind of excited because we had that in common. He already had season tickets and I would not, if we dated, have to drag him to plays or musicals.

Even though I'd vowed not to do any more app chatting or texting, I indulged him because he wanted to text before meeting.

The downside of texting? It takes up time I'd rather spend writing.

The upside of texting? Red flags.

The first was he wanted pictures of me. This constant request I can't figure out. I already determined months ago I was NOT under any circumstances sending nudes. Throwing zero shade on those who do—but that's not me.

I have no body shame and am happy to have sex with the

lights on. But nudes for your phone ain't happening. Last time I checked, the Internet provided plenty of options for men to find naked women of every stripe—for free—in seconds. They did not need to add me to that mix.

Second? He did that thing that drives me batty.

The Married Man: So it occurs to me that perhaps you are on the site to gain material for a book, or are you really here to meet someone? I'm very open minded but it would be nice to know.
Me: OMG that question drives me bat shit crazy. I get it a lot. I honestly have to say that I also write a lot about pedophiles and child sex trafficking, yet no one thinks I'm researching that.
gets off soap box
Honestly my writing life has zero relationship to real life.

That's what I really said, word for word. What I really wanted to say was:

Me: If you have a billion dollars and six pack abs, then yes, I'm doing research.

I didn't though because that wouldn't be nice.

Third red flag? This text after we made a plan to meet up for lunch in West Hollywood.

The Married Man: Also before we meet, I want to give you some up front disclosure in all fairness. I am still married, and my son, wife, and I still live under the same roof. Are you still breathing?
Me: Okay. So what exactly does that mean?
The Married Man: It means I'm still married and I date outside my marriage. Was that a bit too honest?

Me: I'm not sure there's such a thing as too honest.
Does that mean it's open.
The Married Man: No, more of a 'don't ask, don't tell'
situation. We are following the Clintons' lead on this,
LOL. Your thoughts?

At this point it was about eight-thirty at night and I was getting my son through a bath and making sure he used deodorant and that he brushed his teeth thoroughly now that he was out of his first stage of braces and had just been to the dentist to scrape away all that had accumulated in the past few months.

Now I have to be honest. I really wanted to go to lunch with the Married Man. This was a train wreck that I would have loved to see in person. Because *that* would have been freaking fascinating research for a book somewhere down the line that was not romance. I resisted the urge because my goal was a long term relationship and that would have been a huge frolic and detour off the road to what I wanted to be on.

Me: Good morning. I've had time to think about this
(and get much needed sleep of course), and I don't
think we're a match. I have no judgment about open
relationships or DADT or to steal from Dan Savage—
doing what needs to be done to stay married and stay
sane. I'm looking for a serious long term relationship
with someone who is in a similar place as me.
The Married Man: No problem. I certainly understand it's not for everyone! I appreciate your consideration, and I hope you appreciate the full disclosure
upfront. You seem like a wonderful and delightful
person and if you have a change of heart I would love to
meet you. Sincerely, "his real name."

I have so many thoughts few of which are charitable. I will say that I don't consider a week later upfront disclosure. That could have been text number one. The lesson here for me, though, is that I went against my instinct that texting is a horrible waste of my time and going forward, I won't do it again.

THIRTY-SIX

It's Autumn and it's raining

SEPTEMBER 28.

IF I COULD MANIFEST money in the way that I manifest Thunderbolt, I'd be a fucking millionaire.

I'm weak.

I want to be stronger, but I'm not.

My Friday afternoon debate was the same as it always was.

Me: I'm not going to text him. I'm too needy and hate rejection.

Also me: Human connection is important, I can take rejection.

Also me: *texting*

That debate went on for a good four hours. I'm happy to say that at least I wrote a chapter in that span so it wasn't all time wasted. So I sent the needy text and tried that Zen thing everyone in California is into, divorcing oneself from the outcome. My method of doing that was to take a walk and mail a letter that I needed to send.

So I left my apartment and took the ten -minute walk to the post office in West Hollywood. As I walked down the street, I thought to myself, what are the chances of running into Thunderbolt and what would I say if that happened?

The minute I stepped onto the sidewalk in front of the post office, there he was in his new car. I wanted to lift my fist to the universe and tell it that there were a thousand other things I needed and this encounter wasn't one of them.

"You just texted me." That was his opener as I walked by his car.

"I did." I admitted. "How are you?"

I asked about the car, post office nonsense and the like. I decided that if the universe was going to give me a do over, then I was more than happy to ooh and ahh at the car. I took the offer for the four -block ride home. I talked too much while we were in my driveway.

The famous writer's writer Anne Lamott suggests that when we're talking too much we ask ourselves a question in the form of an acronym. "WAIT: Why am I talking?" I swear to God I need to do that because it's such a problem on dates. Not with my friends or family, just with new people I meet and members of the opposite sex. Somewhere in there I shut up enough to hear this question.

"So when are you free?"

"Not until next Thursday."

"So I'll see you Thursday?"

My head nearly exploded. This is someone who told me he could never make plans. That he had to "play it by ear." Then he kissed me in an open convertible in the middle of West Hollywood. I'm going to be honest. I have nowhere to put that.

Where I'm putting that energy is into more dates.

THIRTY-SEVEN

Contrived Quaint

SEPTEMBER 28.

OKAY, I'm burned out on dating energy. I used it all up last night and I'm not at all sure I'll have enough for today. I'm sitting at my laptop right now with tea trying to muster up strength for another date.

Last night was a first date. I'll call him the Soccer Coach, my friends' description wasn't so kind. It's what he does for a school district in the San Fernando valley. It's how he identifies himself on his dating profile. The dating podcasts and books I read over the summer suggested that in order to appear more feminine, women should let men plan dates. Up until now, I'd always been the captain of the dating ship.

So when the Soccer Coach asked me out, I let him take the helm. Which is how I ended up at the Americana Mall in Glendale. It's in a suburb of Los Angeles with a population of about two hundred thousand.

The last two times I was in Glendale were because I needed to buy a birthday present and it has the only Lego store in proximity and it had an Australian based store called Cotton On that's great for Old Navy type prices, but with shirts and pants that not every other kid in my son's class is wearing. Sometimes my son and his classmates looked like little Gap clones, and I liked to mix it up.

The Americana is a Caruso brand location. Rick Caruso is a developer that a lot of people in Southern California have very strong pro and con opinions about.

I'll skip that debate here.

Suffice it to say this mall and the one very close to me, the Grove, seek to mimic small town living, if living in small towns was all retail shops and cable cars that only travel a quarter mile. It's not the kind of place that I frequent.

I met the Soccer Coach in front of the Apple store at seven at night per his request. He led me straight to Coffee Bean & Tea Leaf, a Southern California coffee chain.

He let me order my drink first. He did not offer to pay for it. After I ordered, and the cashier asked if he wanted to order to, he turned to me and said, "Only if we split it." Now, this was a first.

I have a LOT of feelings around someone paying for my meals or coffees. I bounce back and forth between offering to pay and accepting their offer to pay graciously. This was the first time someone left me hanging out there on my own. So I swiped my credit card and paid for the four dollar decaf chai tea latte.

I was too hungry to go the peppermint tea route. Plus I wasn't thinking there was even the remotest possibility of a kiss because, to be honest, he smelled like someone who didn't have a nodding acquaintance with regular shampooing.

He ordered a berry iced tea and we took our drinks to one of the outdoor tables in between the valet stand and the free tram ride that goes back and forth through the mall.

Do you remember Balki Bartokomous the immigrant character from the sitcom *Perfect Strangers*? If not, Google Bronson Pinchot; I'll wait.

I had a childhood crush on him. Our match percentage on

OkCupid was only eighty-two, but he looked like Pinchot, so I had swiped right.

He offered to meet me, but only on weeknights. School nights. I turned down every single one, explaining I was only available on weekends. There were quite a few days of radio silence after that.

When did weekends become so sacred that someone couldn't date on Saturday or Sunday? What exactly are they saving it for? And if their weekends are so precious, then how in the heck would a relationship fit in?

Those questions are purely rhetorical of course. He finally proposed the above meet at the mall on a Saturday night at seven.

Here was my first mistake. I didn't eat lunch or even beforehand. In one of his messages he'd said, let's meet up and go somewhere. I made the mistake of thinking "somewhere" would involve some kind of food. I'd eaten breakfast, done some work, then had gone to a play.

By the time the play ended at five-thirty I was starving. I ran to the Trader Joe's near the theater, bought a Kind bar, scarfed it down and hoped that it would tide me over.

News flash: It didn't.

Half an avocado and an egg are not enough for a day. By the time I pulled into a parking lot after spiraling up for six floors, I was starving. I went back down six escalators toward the Apple store, Instagrammed my usual date photos, then sat by the fountain and waited. Fortunately he found me before I had to go look for him or scrounge for food.

Good news is that he looked like his pictures. Bad news, I'll say that he didn't make much of an effort. I'm starting to think I try too hard. Put on flattering clothes, do my hair, put on jewelry. He showed up in a purple T-shirt, a blue and green plaid flannel, jeans and bright red sneakers.

We got the drinks and sat down—*for three hours.*

For three hours I really tried to engage him. He mostly looked past me, at the kids playing across the way, at the people walking in and out of See's Candies, at what the fuck, I don't know, but not at me or toward me. In all that time, I think he asked me three questions.

One, what did I want out of dating?

Me: long term relationship.

Two, if I worked full time as a writer and traveled, how did I have time for a relationship?

Me: I work from home. I make my own schedule. I'm free every weekend. I have plenty of time.

Three, how could I write books without using dating as research? Where did I get my ideas?

Me: I have a rich inner life.

Yes, I actually said that because I'm over explaining that for me and all the authors I know, ideas are not the limitation, time to write all the books inspired by those ideas is.

The rest of the time I tried to capture his attention. Honestly, I should have left after the first hour. I have no idea why in the hell I was trying so damned hard. The people pleaser in me wanted him to have a good time. I don't know why I felt responsible for his entertainment.

Oh, and that so-called expert's take on OkCupid?

I call bullshit.

I asked the Soccer Coach how he chose whom he wanted to date. His answer, he looks at a picture. That's it. He'd read none of my carefully crafted answers. He did not look at the match percentage. It was just my headshot.

What did I learn in those three hours besides that fact that he finds little kids creepily fascinating? I learned that his longest relationship was six months. In nearly forty years? Six months? Oooh-kay.

He never wanted children. Moved every two years. Had never even committed to a pet. His favorite film was Ghostbusters-the eighties original. He mostly entertained himself on YouTube nightly and only ate out, mainly a diet of spaghetti and rice. He was born and raised in Argentina. Oh and he doesn't date Mexican women.

That's it. That's all I learned.

I took myself home after that. Long ride through the streets of Los Angeles while I tried not to be exhausted by dating. He sent a text while I was in the car on the way home.

Soccer Coach: Thanks for the meeting Jolie, you are very nice. Let me know if you wanna see a movie or get a drink next time.

I ignored that text and the next one a day later. After the third, I told him we weren't a match.

THIRTY-EIGHT

The Hiker

SEPTEMBER 29.

GOT UP. Ate a soft boiled egg. Went to yoga. Took a long shower. Got ready for my second date with The Hiker. If it were up to me, I'd have met for brunch at one of the beach restaurants in Santa Monica or Malibu. The kind with a red vested valet and an obsequious hostess. I'd have dined on a tiny entrée served on beautiful white china on pristine white tablecloths while the waves beat against the sand (Santa Monica) or rocks (Malibu).

Instead, I got this text.

The Hiker: Good morning Jolie, do you like Venice Beach?

Venice Beach.

Remember Zen Guy? Venice Beach.

Remember my second to last date with Classic Car Guy? The one where we'd planned a weekend together, but he left to meet with a private investigator and chase down his kidnapped kids?

Venice Beach.

I should have said something the night before, but I was busy driving to freaking Glendale.

The Hiker: Hi Jolie, What's your availability this weekend?

Me: Good evening! Great to hear from you. I'm free Sunday after yoga. How about you?

The Hiker: That's after 10am, correct? Lunch on Sunday?

Me: Yes after 10. Lunch would be great. Where would you like to meet?

The Hiker: I can come over your way. The Grove, or if you want towards the beach areas?

Me: The beach would be nice. Maybe Santa Monica or Venice or even Marina del Rey...

The Hiker: I will get back to you with a proposal for a location.

Then the next morning, the one above:

The Hiker: Good morning Jolie, Do you like Venice Beach ?

Me: Yes. I actually go walking there fairly often with a friend who lives close by. (This is true, but we usually walk along the strand south of the tourist and busker filled Muscle Beach area).

The Hiker: Great. What time is good for you? I will be very casual, blue jeans and tennis shoes.

Me: 11 onwards. About to leave for yoga. Let me know what works and I'll meet you there.

The Hiker: Let's say 12:00

After yoga, he still hadn't pinned down a location. Planning was weirdly hard for these guys.

Me: okay. Perfect. Let me know where you'd like to meet. I have to head out soon in order to get across town in time.

The Hiker: Let's meet at the main restaurant on the boardwalk. I forgot the name. Next to the souvenir shop Lalaland. I will call you when I have parked.

So one thing I've learned about myself as I age is that I'm a planner. I really, really hate last minute plans. I did it with Classic Car Guy because he really gave me no choice. Sex with the emotionally unavailable hawt guy came at a price I was willing to pay. With the Hiker, not so much.

So I took my no plan anxious self from West Hollywood to Venice. Once you get past a street called Abbott Kinney, Venice becomes crowded with narrow streets and parking from hell. Eighteen dollar parking from hell.

While I was on Venice Boulevard about a half mile from the Pacific Ocean, I got a text.

He'd pulled into a lot near the beach and was happy to pay my parking. I took him up on the offer. I only had twelve dollars in my wallet, enough for valet plus tip, not enough for self-parking. It was a kind offer. He met me there and we walked to the beach. If you check out the pictures on Instagram from that date, you'll recognize it. It's the corner where I met Zen Guy. The restaurant was the same one where I ate with Classic Car Guy. Venice isn't big enough for my dating adventures.

So we walked and ate at the Sidewalk Café. I ordered the same salad as before. Like Classic Car Guy, the Hiker got pasta. What in the hell was up with that?

I ate. I was funny and charming. He mentioned that he

didn't eat condiments or salad dressing. Liked his food plain. He paid for lunch. He carried my stuff. He listened to all of my crazy theories on the brain's neuroplasticity and writing.

I was the "real girl." He told me that he was shy and introverted. I learned that he'd been married. Was stepfather to two children who were now parents themselves and back in Denmark.

One of my super powers is reading people. It works with ninety percent of the population. It doesn't work with people of the opposite sex when I'm interested in them. (Which is why it completely didn't work on Classic Car Guy or Thunderbolt—they remain completely opaque to me.) But it worked well on the Hiker. It would not be too much to say that he was quite charmed by me.

What in the hell did I do with that?

I swear to God, if he were ten years younger, I might give it a try. Now I'm stuck with a guy who's lovely. Who I'd probably like if he were younger and a film maker or author. Not a logistical expert in moving stuff from one part of the world to another in shipping containers. I talked a lot about my love of artists. So when I got home I had a text from him.

The Hiker: Jolie, I enjoy our conversations a lot.

This was followed by pictures from the top of some mountain as well as beautiful slides of the Disney concert hall in downtown L.A., Niagara Falls, and a sunset over the ocean. Also pictures from the snowy peak of some mountain. The place where he says he finds Zen.

I talked to some friends. I went to a movie. Then I texted back—four hours later. Yes, if Thunderbolt had texted, I'd have replied in less than a few seconds.

Me: Wow these pictures are amazing. I have to say I'm

partial to the last three. I'll take your word on the Zen of the mountains. Thanks so much for the lunch and conversation. I had a good time.

All of that was true. I put down my phone then got on my laptop and Googled what to do you when you catch feelings for your friend with benefits/fuck buddy.

THIRTY-NINE

The Art Show

OCTOBER 4.

BEFORE WE GET to the show, there was a little blip in my promise to myself to not do a hookup. I fell off the wagon on Thursday night.

He was an artist. He was hot. Like L.A. actor hot. Actually L.A. actor hot because he's an L.A. Actor. Think Brad Pitt during Thelma and Louise. I couldn't say no. If he's ever that famous, well...I can say I knew him when.

He came over. It was good. Thunderbolt was busy, and I needed to put all that energy somewhere.

When that was all done, I came back to my senses and tried to figure out how I was going to navigate Friday night.

According to my artist friend, I'll call her Pierce, we'd known each other sixteen years. I'm not good with timelines after moving from the east coast to Southern California. In the land of perpetual summer, there are few markers of years passing.

We'd met in a writing class that I think was lovingly called, Finish the D*mned Book. It was a lifesaver because it actually helped me finish my first book. I remember going to one of her early art shows at a gallery in Eagle Rock. So this huge show, where she was on the cover of the gallery catalog was a really big deal.

I was so much looking forward to seeing her and spending some quality time with her. Here's where I made my mistake. I sent this text to the Hiker on Wednesday morning.

Me: Morning! On Friday night I'm going to my friend's opening gallery reception in Redondo Beach. If you're free, I'd love for you to join me there.

The Hiker should have been receiving a kiss off text and not this missive from me. I sent it because I felt guilty for not liking someone who'd been nice to me. I sent it because I didn't want him to feel like he'd wasted his time. Even as I write this now, my motivations don't really make much sense. The moment I sent the text, I regretted it. I wanted to take it back, but he replied immediately.

The Hiker: I would love to. I do have another thing Friday evening. Let me check if this will still happen or if I cancel it.

I wanted to text back, "No! Don't cancel! Do your thing." I sent back nothing.

There is no magic teleportation device between West Hollywood and the beach communities. On Friday night, I'd have loved one. Instead, I hunkered down in my SUV with music, podcasts, and audiobooks for the hour plus long ride ninety-five percent of which would be on surface streets because not only is there no teleportation device between the two cities, there's no freeway either.

While I was driving I got a text from the Hiker that he was on his way and he'd be there around seven -forty. I hustled and got there by quarter after seven. I needed space to prep Pierce and myself. I wanted to show up fully for my friend, so I was more dressed up than usual. I had on a little black dress, courtesy of Calvin Klein, some very cute heels that I'd unearthed from the back of my closet by mistake while I was searching for something else this week, and most importantly, Spanx. It sucked in my post baby body and made me almost look young again.

My friend had a lot of support that night. We were all talking in a group about how we knew Pierce, when I saw the Hiker drift by. I caught his eye, but he didn't come over. Somehow he seemed overwhelmed by all of us. He was wearing a gray button down, a gray sweater vest and maybe even gray pants. He exists in a completely different L.A. than I do, where men wear ripped seven hundred dollar jeans, T-shirts on par with that, and Chukkas (men's leather ankle boots).

I wondered if it was his Danish roots. Either way, he was walking in his loafers toward another exhibit space. Couldn't figure out the etiquette. Should I run after him to show him how happy I was that he came? Or was I to leave him to his own devices so I could observe him, like an animal in the zoo, to see how he handled this social situation?

Hesitation made the decision for me. I talked to my friends and talked up Pierce when serious collectors strolled by.

Eventually, the Hiker came back. I introduced him around, then went off to look at art with him. His favorites were all cityscapes and beach -themed paintings. Either mostly black or brown, tan, green, and blue canvases.

I'm sure it will come as no surprise to you that I loved the intriguing black and white photos, the art with bright pops of color, sculptures with heft and dimension.

Did I mention that during our lunch the previous week, the Hiker mentioned that he doesn't eat condiments or salad dressing? He liked his food plain, he said. His tastes in art mirrored his tastes in food.

Eventually we came back to Pierce. More friends of hers poured in, and our conversation got livelier and more fun. There was copious wine.

I was enjoying myself so much that it took me a good half hour before I realized that he wasn't among us. He'd found a seat and was paging through the catalog.

Again, I felt like I needed to try to bring him into the conversation, introduce him to another hobbyist photographer or get his opinion on musical theater. Again I let the opportunity pass. Maybe he was way more introverted than me and this was too much.

I excused myself from the group one last time and did a second swing through a different part of the gallery with the Hiker. Abruptly at nine-thirty on the dot, he announced that he had to leave straight away.

Not wanting to feel later like I'd been unkind, I followed him out to the lot. We were parked only a few cars apart. We stood awkwardly talking about the show for two or three minutes.

Have you ever felt yearning coming off another person in waves? That's what this was like. The ball was in my court. I could have leaned in and hugged him, kissed him, or touched him, and it would have been welcome. I wanted to try to satisfy what I felt were his desires, but I also didn't want to send the wrong kind of signal. Instead, I shifted from foot to foot while holding extra catalogs against my chest like a middle school student.

Eventually I prompted a goodbye. We hugged, he bussed me on the cheek, then he strode to his car.

I swapped out my heels for my Uggs and hopped up into my own car.

I was happy not to hear from him for a few hours. Saturday morning I got this text.

The Hiker: Hi Jolie. I hope your day is going well. I enjoyed our time last night. It reminded me that I need to up my game on galleries, which I really like. I am running errands today and preparing for my hike next week. I look forward to speaking with you again soon. The Hiker

After the gym, I downloaded with a couple of girlfriends whose opinions I value. These two never see eye to eye.

One friend said I should just dump him now. There were other fish in the sea. On the Hiker's standoffishness, she was on the fence. On the one hand, he could just be a party pooper. On the other, she said, maybe he's just mature, found a way to amuse himself because he didn't like groups, and regulated his actions. That sounded all mature and shit. But so much of my social life is big group stuff with chatting and sparkly conversation and often wine. Would he be over in a corner looking quiet at every occasion? Or did he like his social life like his liked his food, no spice, no condiments, just interacting with the person he was dating?

My other friend sent over a Diahann Carroll (who died yesterday, RIP. When I went to Google the spelling of her name, I realized she'd died. I don't know what that says about my friend's sense of humor or lack thereof.) GIF where the actress tosses over her shoulder the caption TRY HARDER; "with the Hiker" went unspoken. She liked his texts and thought that if I hung in there, attraction and desire could grow.

My next few weeks were wall to wall busy. Instead of responding to the Hiker, I got on Bumble, swiped right and made a date for Sunday.

FORTY

Dating Outside my Neighborhood

OCTOBER 7.

CAN we get to how the night ended? Spoiler Alert: It ended like many of my first dates ended, with Thunderbolt at my house.

"It was so weird running into you," he said while we were talking about what happened in the days we'd been apart.

"Did I freak you out?" I asked. It had freaked *me* out a little —or a lot.

"No. We live really close, huh?" I knew that "no" was a lie. I would have said exactly the same thing if he'd asked.

"Yes, we do," I acknowledged. "Yes we do."

Which was why the last few dates had been far from West Hollywood. Last night's date lived, ironically, in my old neighborhood. Since my ex had my kid and hates eating out—or at least he always complained about leaving our house because most restaurant food wasn't all organic and made from locally sourced ingredients like he demanded from me—eating out for him didn't used to be a pleasure for anyone involved. So I felt safer down the street from my old house than near West Hollywood.

Let's call last night's date the Late Bloomer. He said it

239

enough times for it to have stuck in my mind. I decided to meet at a local gastro pub some friends owned. It had great drinks, great bar food, and was open until two, so if the date was going well, there would be no pressure to leave.

It started like they all do. I was on time. He was late, even though he only had to travel a mile or two.

Late Bloomer: I'm on my way and may be a few minutes late.
Me: I'm here.

Fortunately for me, I'd brought a book or a hundred. Thank goodness for the Kindle. That device is how I (maybe pretended) entertained myself with dates who were late—which was all of them.

I'd taken a stool at a high table. Considered the drink menu. People watched. About fifteen minutes later, he made it to the bar/restaurant. He was wearing a long -sleeved dark shirt, jeans. He didn't look at me, but everywhere but me instead.

Another one, I thought. Why is it that no one could look me in the eye?

"I usually have to work at night. It's a rare night off," he said.

"What do you do?"

"I'm the vault manager at one of the city's theaters."

"What's that?" I asked. I'd never thought of the city's venues having a vault.

"I'm in charge of collecting, counting, and depositing the cash after concerts," he said. "I'm pretty important to the organization. Unfortunately my new boss won't give me a future schedule, so I'm not always sure which nights I have off."

Now of course, I'm going to tell you, that his bio focused

not on cash collection, but how he was a writer and lover of fiction. I love creative people.

"Do you get to see interesting concerts?" I asked.

He named a few bands I'd never heard of. "But the season ends in a few weeks."

"Why?"

"The city closes its outside venues during the rainy season," he explained.

I realized that I'd forgotten that places like the Hollywood Bowl were closed during months when there was even the possibility of rain.

"Do you write during the down time?" I asked.

"I want to write," he said. "I used to write short stories and I have my own blog, but I don't have time." I didn't probe how seven months off between mid -October and mid -May seemed like a ton of time to work on short stories.

He asked me about my own writing. I told him I'd recently finished a book and was working on another. I talked a little about romance, but didn't want to talk about 'research' or answer his questions on what I thought about erotica.

"How did you come to Los Angeles?" I asked. It was like pulling teeth to get answers. Conversation wasn't flowing smoothly, though, and I'd already invested thirty minutes in driving and was drinking sparkling rosé. I needed at least an hour and a half before I could safely drive home.

"The first time?" he asked.

I leaned across the gray washed wood table. Now this sounded like it could be an interesting story.

"Yes, the first time."

"I went to film school and came out here to be in entertainment. It was two thousand two. Eventually, I lost my job in the economic downturn and ran out of money. I was...well I don't want to get into it, but I was partying a lot. I have to...I think I need to tell you something."

That phrase is a killer. Whenever it's spoken, I'm both equal parts intrigued and afraid. I took a sip of wine, leaned in a little more.

"Do you know what autism is?"

I sat back a little. I nodded.

He continued. "I'm on the spectrum with Asperger's. I have a hard time with conversation and talking to people, but I'm a lot better than I used to be."

I have to say, first, I didn't see that coming and second, I didn't quite know what to say back to that. I'd read a bit about neuroatypical or neurodivergent people and the need for neurotypicals to be more accepting of people with different types of brains. I didn't think, though, that I was ready to date someone who was struggling with socialization. I'd had that debate only two nights before.

Not so subtly, I checked my phone. The "do not disturb" was on. I turned it off because I wanted to see Thunderbolt and figured I'd miss his text if I wasn't vigilant.

Late Bloomer talked about how he hadn't lost his virginity until his twenties, but he hadn't had a lot of luck with girl-friends. He'd worked at Waldenbooks back in the day, and was currently reading Daphne DuMaurier and Fyodor Dostoevsky. New books, ebooks didn't interest him. The same was true about movies. He was lamenting the closure of the silent movie theater two years ago.

What are my dates' obsessions with the past? Classic Car Guy loved his sixties cars and seventies music. The Soccer Coach only watched the movies from the eighties that he could find on YouTube. And now this one was lamenting on the introduction of ebooks into a paper world.

After that, he talked about Frank Zappa for the remainder of the time. He loved the musician's complicated work. What I know about Zappa...you know what? I don't know a damned thing about Zappa except that he lived in Laurel Canyon and that his sons were feuding over his music catalog. I made the mistake of mentioning the latter.

While I drank a quart of water, Late Bloomer talked about Zappa's bandmates, his children, and innumerable other facts about the music legend.

Even though I knew it was rude, I glanced at my phone again.

Silent.

"I have to get going," I announced a bit abruptly. "I have an early class at the gym."

"Gym. What do you do?"

"Spinning at eight," I said.

"So you work out a few times a week?"

"Sure. Spinning. Yoga."

"I've heard of spinning," he said.

"It's just indoor cycling to music," I replied.

"Well it seems to agree with you," he said looking me up and down. I pulled my oversized cardigan over my form-fitting velvet mock T. I mean I get it about men being visual. An hour later, Thunderbolt would be pulling off my bra because he couldn't see my breasts during foreplay. Most men, however, wouldn't have said it quite that way, not unless it was a hookup type date.

"I'm about ready to call it a night," I said. I flagged down the waiter and asked for the bill.

"Can you stay a few more moments? I want to go to the restroom."

I nodded and checked my phone again. There was a text, but this one was from an author friend who was nervous about her new release. I broke all my rules about no phone on dates and texted her back. I was fiddling with my phone when he came back.

He paid for his two glasses of wine and my one. I thanked him and stood.

"Can I walk you to your car?" he asked.

It was only in the back, so I nodded. This wouldn't be as long a walk as it had been with others.

"Here I am," I said in the few seconds it took us to walk out of the back door.

"I really like you. Can we see each other again?"

That took me aback. It was the least subtle profession of interest that I'd heard. Because I hate confrontation, I had no idea what to say.

"I hope I didn't talk too much," he continued, "or fixate on any one thing too much. I'm really trying to learn how to relate to people. So?"

"I'm busy the next couple of weeks," I said. "Let's keep in touch."

"Please text me and let me know you got home safely."

"Sure. No problem," I promised.

Then I backed out of the space like a bat out of hell and took myself over Laurel Canyon. My phone pinged.

Thunderbolt: Oh hi.
Me: How are you?
Thunderbolt: Mellow.
Me: Did you say mellow? Siri is reading your texts because I'm driving.
Thunderbolt: You wanna fool around?
Me: Sure. I'll be home in ten minutes.
Thunderbolt: Here.
Me: Really?

That *really* was because I'd only been home a couple of minutes before he'd pulled up next to my car in the new convertible. I hadn't gotten more than my shoes off. The rest of me was still in full date wear.

I was honestly delighted to see him because it was easy.

There were no moments of awkward conversation or me having to explain anything about my life. Plus he was currently obsessed with G-spot orgasms. So we were all good.

You know, of course, that I forgot to text Late Bloomer. I also got a text from The Hiker that I didn't respond to either. I needed to clear the decks, but I didn't know how. Instead, I napped with Thunderbolt, then sent him on his way with enough time to make his six AM flight.

In the morning after the gym, I put the final touches on a book before it went to my editor.

Writing was easy.

Dating was hard.

FORTY-ONE

Sick Days

OCTOBER 12-13.

ALL OF A SUDDEN my interest in dating has dropped to zero. I took myself to the gym, to yoga, to a play, and home to binge watch Netflix this weekend and oddly, it was all quite satisfying. I even had an exchange with Thunderbolt that didn't involve talking about sex we'd had, sex with other people, or sex we'd have in the future.

> **Me:** I keep forgetting to text you...you left sunglasses here. Hope you're enjoying Nashville.
> **Thunderbolt:** Oh, thanks. Yeah all's well out here.
> **Me:** 'well' seems like an understatement. Was scrolling through IG as one does (but doesn't admit publicly even under pain of death) and congrats are in order.
> **Thunderbolt:** Aww...thanks

His film had won a couple more awards and had been chosen for another prestigious festival.

That was enough.

Just so you know, I haven't forgotten that I've fallen for my FWB. Trust me, I've gamed it out in my head a few or a thousand times—mostly while driving, which gives me entirely too much space and time to think.

If I told Thunderbolt I had feelings for him, there was no way I could see it going well. He'd already said more than once that he wasn't interested in a relationship. I could try reading a lot into his behavior, but if I learned anything with Classic Car Guy, it was to pay attention to a mismatch between words and actions.

Classic Car Guy's words were all "yes," but his standing me up said "no."

Thunderbolt's actions were all "yes," but his words said "no."

See that?

Mismatch.

I've been burned once. I can't walk down that road again.

I'm not sure what I'm doing that's not working with men, but I'm taking a hiatus from it.

Getting sick helped a lot. I was supposed to be out today with a new guy. I'll call him The Hotel Guy. He's from the same place that I summer. It was a delight to text with someone who knew about my other life. I was kind of interested to meet him, not just for dating, but to talk about life in another country. That was until he asked me to meet him at a hotel...

Full disclaimer here. The Hotel Guy's texts are translated from another language. Classic Car Guy's often were as well. I speak two languages other than English.

The Hotel Guy: HELLO Jolie. How are you today? I don't have a Car right now Because I've sold it But I'm looking for another one in a Month I'll have My car again. I'd like to ask You please if Your can come to where I live and pay for You gasoline! Unfortunately I will only have My car in about

Three weeks! What do You think Jolie? Have a
Wonderful day!

Me: I can meet you on the Westside. Why don't you
choose the place and I can meet you there around 2
or so.

The Hotel Guy: [he gave me the address of a
boutique hotel] This is my address. Have a nice afternoon. What do you think Jolie?

Me: I'm just home from the theater. Let's talk tomorrow. Where you are would be a long drive. Maybe we
can meet in Santa Monica. It's a bit closer for me and a
short Uber ride for you, I think....

Then I woke up sneezing and sniffly and texted him that I
was too sick to meet. He said I should have tea with honey. I
was on my second mug by the time I read his text.

The other prospective dates?

Cute guy, long hair, interesting job... He was looking for
reality show prospects:

Casting Director: Hi Jolie! Thanks for writing me
back!! My name is Dan and I am a Casting Producer
here in L.A.. I am working on a home renovation show
for HGTV. It is an amazing show with talented
designer [I'm omitting the star's name]! So I am here
looking for newly single homeowners that are ready to
renovate the home they lived in with their ex. If this is
you I would love to chat! Hope to hear back!

I didn't reply back that I'd moved out. That I didn't get the
house because I didn't want to live in a place with bad
memories.

Next up was the Playwright. He lived in Orange County
but said he was willing to drive because he was dying to meet

me. I'd said sure then left the ball in his court. On Saturday he sent a text.

Playwright: Hope we can meet. I would like to pick your brain on crafting an interesting play. I could use some information as to how to build believable conflict between my lead characters.

Nope, I don't want to help him write his play. Fortunately he was busy with his kids, so I'll bet that meeting will never happen.

The others. Pen pals. If they don't want to meet in person, I don't do the texting thing. So lots of lovely connections with lovely people, but not one of them wanted to meet so there was nothing to be done about that.

Last week I was thinking about hiring a dating coach. Even had a call with one, but decided I wasn't willing to plunk down eight thousand dollars (I know, right?!) for eight weeks of coaching. I'm not sure that's the answer. Right now I don't know what it is, but I think I'm going to spend a couple of months thinking about how to change.

In the meantime, as I'm typing this I've just received a text from the Hiker. He sent beautiful pictures from his hike in the Sierras. Last week I was lamenting how to let the Hiker down. My therapist assures me that after three dates I don't owe him anything. When and if he asked me out again, she assured me I can tell him that we're not a match and leave it at that.

I wasn't looking forward to that.

FORTY-TWO

Honesty

OCTOBER 17.

I GOT a text from the Hiker this afternoon. I was busy driving around town picking up random items for a weekend camping trip with my son. It's an annual tradition at his school. More than a hundred students and their parents leave our comfortable climate controlled homes to drive three hours east into the mountains where we'll sleep and eat rough. The kids will run wild. The adults will day drink.

The Hiker: How are you doing today?

A couple of hours later, when I had a moment in the school parking lot, I replied.

Me: I'm mostly great. I'm packing for a weekend camping trip. Starts tomorrow. How are you?

He's not a texter. Something about being fifty-seven has no doubt kept him out of the world of texting.

I know that I need to let him off the hook and send him on his way to find his counterpart, but I haven't.

This has been my 'come to Jesus' week. I've spent a lot of time excavating my craven heart. My conclusion: I'm the asshole. It was humbling to think that I haven't been nice to everyone I've dated, mainly Thunderbolt. He's had his own asshole moments, don't get me wrong, but I haven't been kind. In fact, I realize I've been very cavalier with his feelings. I don't know what those feelings are because god knows, he's pretty awful at expressing them. After I texted the hiker, I took a deep breath and made a decision.

I sent this text to Thunderbolt.

Me: Hey there. I was just thinking about you. Are you in town Sunday night? I'm leaving for a weekend camping trip tomorrow morning, but would love to see you if you're free.

It felt more vulnerable to type that than it looks on the screen.

FORTY-THREE

There are no happy endings

OCTOBER 21.

ONCE A YEAR I go camping with my son. The upside? Lots of time to hang out and bond. The downside is that there's no cell service. At all. Not even kidding. There are places in California where there are no cell towers.

Usually it's a relief. This weekend not so much. In addition to setting up and sleeping a tent. Hiking. Biking and the like, I spun out in my head. I know all the advice now is about not dwelling on the past or future, but my mind was not on board.

Yesterday afternoon, driving down the mountain was like being in trial and waiting for a verdict. Mine? Ghosted. Thunderbolt read my text and opted not to reply. That's the first time ever I haven't gotten a reply text.

But late afternoon, I had to drop my kid at his dad's house. I avoid my ex like the plague. I'm never in the mood for a lecture on what's wrong with me, what I've done wrong, how I've ruined all our lived or some variation of the above. We still share the camping equipment, however, and my old house has acres of storage while my little West Hollywood spot doesn't.

After I unloaded my SUV, (No he didn't help. He's not the kind of guy who would do that. He just stood by arms folded watching me move tent, sleeping bags, and all the rest of it) he gave me a look I dreaded. It was him crying.

"How are you?" he asked.

It wasn't at all what I'd prepared for. My mind was filled with thoughts of whether my son had caught a cold, whether I had time for a car wash, and what I'd say to Thunderbolt if I saw him. Not one of those was about my ex.

"As good as can be expected," I replied.

Obviously he was no longer privy to the ups and downs of my life. Then he did the thing I hadn't heard in several months. He begged for reconciliation, a second chance, therapy, anything.

Like I do for dates that go on too long, I indulged him. Letting him emote all over the garage. Then I turned my back, closed the garage, got into my SUV and left. I did drive down to the car wash, which is another thirty or forty minutes of waiting and thinking. Los Angeles is always good for that.

My life was dominated by mismatches. Men who wanted me, I didn't want them. The more I wanted them, the less they wanted me. Something was broken. Last week I thought I had clarity. Now I knew that I really didn't.

Sunday night was hard. I turned down a repeat performance from the Actor while I waited in vain for some acknowledgement. If you've read this far, I'm sure you know that I don't do silence well. I couldn't take it from Classic Car guy and I'd never experienced it from Thunderbolt. But there it was.

So I turned out all the lights, slipped into bed, and tried to enjoy *The Mistake* from Elle Kennedy. (It's really good). Before I drifted off, I sent one last text. I *know. I* know. I can't help myself sometimes or all the time.

Me: Hi. Long weekend in the mountains without cell

service. I'm heading to bed. There's something I want
to talk to you about. Let me know when you're free.

I know that it was probably too little too late, but I can't
say that I tried at least a tiny bit to stick my toe in the water.

That said, continuing to string the Hiker along is not nice,
so I'm going to stop doing that. Going to text him this
morning that we're not a match.

That's it. Back out on the market again...maybe. I really
enjoy dating. But it's exhausting me. Maybe I need to do something else with my weekends.

In the meantime, there will be some regression. Going to
take the Actor for another spin. This time, though, I'm going
to be one hundred percent clear up front what I want from
him which is nothing more than a good time. Ambiguity has
not been my friend.

FORTY-FOUR

Fall Back

The Hiker: Hi Jolie. I would love to meet again. Are you available in the near future?
Me: Hi again. It was great to connect with you. While I've enjoyed getting to know you, I've decided to date someone else exclusively. I did not want to leave anything open ended. I wish only good things for you going forward.

THAT WAS A PARTIAL TRUTH. Deciding that I *wanted* to be exclusive with Thunderbolt wasn't exactly the same as being exclusive with him. Either way I'd been honest that I didn't want to date him.

After that I opened my phone. Disabled my Bumble profile. Went away indefinitely from OKCupid. Took myself out of the Tinder stack.

I'm not meeting my people. Creative. Secure. Confident. Open to a relationship. When I'd started on this journey, I'd thought it was a numbers game. Now, I'm not so sure.

On Friday, while I was trying to work out my dating and divorce frustrations in yoga, Thunderbolt texted that he was back in town on Sunday. While I debated on what to say to him, I did more yoga. I did some spinning. I spent time with a writer friends who's leaving Southern California for the northern part of the state. I went to see a Pulitzer prize winning play at the Fountain Theater.

Then Sunday night came. I spun around my apartment cleaning an already clean space, folding clothes, putting various items in a Goodwill bag. Two weeks ago I'd been all gung ho to talk to Thunderbolt. By Sunday, I'd lost most of my nerve.

Which maybe a friend could see, because while we were driving home from lunch, she told me there's nothing wrong with kicking the 'Determine the Relationship' talk down the road.

I didn't do that exactly. There were so many mental health reasons why that wasn't a good idea. I couldn't spend any more time spinning out scenarios in my mind and remain sane.

So promptly as always, Thunderbolt showed up on Sunday night bottle of wine in hand. I can't decide if he'd leveled up his entire wardrobe or just dressed better when he was at my house. It's odd actually given that at least half of the time he isn't dressed at all. Maybe all the showering and snappy dressing was wasted.

Anyway, after I poured the wine and invited him to sit on my banquette—which is my favorite perch in my apartment nowadays, I paused, took a breath and launched in the only way I could figure.

"So the thing I said I wanted to talk about?"

"Yeah."

"In October I kind of had a 'come to Jesus' moment where I decided I needed to apologize for some asshole behavior I'd engaged in earlier this year. You see, I kind of pride myself on always being kind and I think I was unkind."

He looked perplexed. "No, I think you're always kind."

"Well I don't think so. I wanted to say that I was sorry for involving you in my dating life. It wasn't my best moment."

"It was no big deal," Thunderbolt said. "Didn't bother me in the least. We have a non exclusive, non monogamous, casual thing, right? I don't mind hearing about your other partners. It may even turn me on a little bit."

I took a slow blink. Held up my wine glass. Took a sip. Didn't believe any of the bullshit he'd shoveled. But there was nothing but to take it at face value.

Took another sip. Changed the subject. Talked about something else. I couldn't square away what he said with how he acted. But I decided that I didn't have to. We moved on to a chat about Milwaukee, the perils of O'Hare, his upcoming trip to Fresno, and the cub scouts in 1986.

There was this moment, though, that was a bit of an out of body experience. He was standing in the middle of my bedroom completely naked. I have no idea when he'd shed all his clothes. I was standing on the other side messing around with a lamp. This singular moment was the only time he was truly vulnerable. He was great to talk to about almost anything except feelings because that's where the vulnerability ended.

I recently read in a book that the qualities that annoy you about someone are the qualities that you don't like in yourself. In this case, I think it's true.

If I ask Thunderbolt anything about how he feels there's so much deflection and denial, it's legendary. I know that feeling and it's something I hate about myself and something I want to change more than anything.

Several hours later when I was walking him out my back door, he looked back at me.

"Safe travels," I said.

"So, I'll see you when I land from Fresno?"

"I'll be here," I said. Because I would. I knew that as well as I knew my name.

One of my friends—they all hate him for me, don't worry —asked me if I was in love with Thunderbolt. The answer was no. I don't really have the words though for person who takes up way too much space in my brain.

My friend and I went back and forth about why I spend time with someone who behaves like this with me. I didn't have a good answer. Maybe because I like crumbs. Because I feel comfortable where I don't have to deal with any demands or real emotions. If I were a betting person, that's where I'd put my money. Later, she sent over unsolicited advice. She said that I need people in my life who love Jolie for Jolie, who appreciate me and don't take me for granted.

Two days later, I got this text from the Hiker.

The Hiker: Hi Jolie. I appreciate your message although I was hoping for a better outcome. Don't shy back from contacting me for any Danish details that you could possibly use in your writing. If in any way, I could be your friend. I would find that a treasure in itself. Have a great evening. The Hiker.

Yes, I know that I gave up lovely and nice and honest and appreciates me and doesn't take me for granted for ambiguous and emotionally unavailable.

That's where I'm at right now. Hopefully in a few weeks or a few months, I'll fix all of that. I want to be different and want different things. It's a matter of figuring out how to get there.

FORTY-FIVE

Tantric Speed Dating

THE BEST WAY TO get to fifty first dates? Do twenty in one Saturday night...

Obsessing over Thunderbolt was yielding me nothing. I saw him the day before I flew to a romance writer's conference in Houston. It was the only time I'd have available in the upcoming weeks and I wanted to see him. Rather than the back and forth texting between us that I'd grown to dislike, I took my friend's advice and not only was I one hundred percent myself, I asked for what I wanted.

> **Me:** I'm flying to Houston this week for a week. I'd love to see you later tonight if you're free...
> **Thunderbolt:** I think that could work.

After that it was just logistics and I got what I wanted, time with him.

Then I traveled. To Houston. To Crystal Beach. To the big island of Hawaii. I was anywhere but Southern California. I had a birthday with friends as I face down middle age. And in all that I missed Thunderbolt. I missed his humor, his easy conversation, and obviously the sex. It was, has been the best of my life.

To paraphrase Brianna Wiest, what we don't like about other people is what we don't like about ourselves. The whatever (situationship) I have with Thunderbolt has been a ruthless reflection. While away (and during nearly eighteen hours of flying) I had some time to journal. I took the time to write down the things that drive me bat shit crazy about Thunderbolt. Here they are:

One.

He never compliments me. It was the thing I liked about Classic Car Guy. It was probably what walked me into a relationship with him. After this spring, I realized that it was something I enjoyed. It made me feel good. Thunderbolt doesn't excel at that. At least not with me. While I was away I spent some time trying to think if he'd ever said anything positive. What I could recall is that he said I didn't look as old at my age. After I lost twenty pounds on the divorce diet, he said that my body looked good. When I asked him why he'd swiped right, he said it was because I was attractive. That's it.

Then I held up that ruthless mirror. Because I wondered if I'd ever complimented him. I nearly came up blank. There was, of course, my opening salvo. The thing I messaged to him over Tinder. Last week, though I realized that I need to give what I want. So when he appeared in a nice shirt (again?!), I complimented him. In nine months it was the only nice thing I remember saying.

Two.

His communication is opaque. Because he texts me. Because he's here, I have to assume that he wants to spend time with me. He's never said that, though. Instead his texts are all 'hi' and 'are you in town.' I've been better about being direct because the other is mentally exhausting. It's been better. Not perfect. But better.

Three.

He never says what he feels. He talks around a subject whenever I ask any question that touches on how he feels about something. Of course, I've never said a thing about how I feel about him. The thought of saying anything nice seems like I'd be walking on the third rail.

When I was going to say something in October, I completely lost my nerve. He talked about the casual non monogamous nature of the thing we have. That kept me quiet. Because who would want to say anything in the face of that declaration. It's bothering me though, not saying anything. I can't say why. Of course I'm having all these thoughts on the heels of reading a self help book that suggests—like they all do —that if I put my energy into this situationship, then I won't be open to meeting anyone who really fulfills what I want and need.

The mirror, though, is not flattering.

"One other important note is that research shows people are attracted to those who are on par with their own communication abilities. This means that if you have difficulty communicating, you may be attracted to others who also have impaired communication skills and less attracted to those who have the ability to communicate better than you do." Weber, Jill P. Having Sex, Wanting Intimacy (p. 104). Rowman & Littlefield Publishers.

So his awful communication style is a reflection of mine. Men who communicate better probably wouldn't find me attractive. Or maybe I'd be intimidated by them. My therapist said that I'm probably not quite ready for that 'big love' relationship I want. She also said that if I'm honest with myself and Thunderbolt then either we will grow together or I'll outgrow him. But he's good practice.

Rather than reach out to him about being back in town and wanting to see him, because that's would be my joy, I googled 'speed dating' while I was in Hawaii. I found an event the night after I landed and signed up for the last available spot.

The event was in Silverlake, a cute community on the east side of Los Angeles. I left my apartment in West Hollywood, even though I was tired from landing late and chasing down lost luggage. Even though I was tired from not enough sleep and it was a cold and rainy night, I drove the twenty five minutes into the dating unknown.

There were about twenty five men and twenty women. They tried to keep the numbers even, but men's tickets sold out first, and several women were no shows. That's a thing in Los Angeles. Rain keeps people inside.

I went in blind. At the registration desk the facilitator handed me a pouch filled with beads. It tiny beaded letters in it. My letter was 'M.'

The men's pouches were empty. She inscribed that twelfth letter of the alphabet next to my name on a list and welcomed me. We went into the room, a large one inside a yoga studio. The middle of the room featured a colorful blanket with a picture of one of the Hindu goddesses as well as candles. We each grabbed a blanket and sat in a circle waiting for instruction. We opened with deep breathing exercises, then she explained what would happen this evening.

We'd engage in one minute Tantric exercises with each man. Then he'd close his eyes and we'd put a bead in if we were interested or not if we weren't.

Like Bumble, it was a women's choice night. So breathed deep and got ready to start. I met twenty five different men. I danced with some, hugged others, looked into their eyes, and tried to make a connection. I gave beads to a few. Interestingly several were people I'd have swiped left on online, but who were engaging in real life when they were animated, and more than pictures and words on a page. It was a surprisingly good time. It was different than driving or walking to coffee or whatever someone hadn't planned.

As I type this, an email has come in with a list of the people I matched with. I haven't clicked on the link.

Now I have to make the first move or wait for them to. I haven't looked at the list yet because I don't feel as open to the possibilities as I want to be. Part of me, a large part unfortunately, feels like I need to settle something with Thunderbolt before I attempt to make any other connections.

I worry that I'll do what I've been doing all along—allowing myself to keep things superficial on dates because I know that I can always come home to Thunderbolt and it will be joyful and fun and will keep me from focusing on anything else with anyone new.

I don't want a new person to become TGIUTAFATOG (the guy I use to avoid feelings about the other guy). That would be a repeat of the very same mistake. Then I'd be on a hamster wheel. I wasn't ready to repeat the cycle.

FORTY-SIX

The Physical Therapist

DECEMBER 6.

I HAVE to wonder if this is some evolution. Instead of dating people who are either super attractive, but emotionally unavailable or who are generally good looking, but sane, I appear to be moving toward the latter.

Today I had my first coffee date with a guy from tantric speed dating. He grew up just east of Los Angeles. Has a normal family, friends, a fourteen year old daughter.

Now, I'm gonna be honest, I started the date like I ended others, thinking about Thunderbolt. While I was waiting for Mr. PT to get to Starbucks, yes he was forty-five minutes late —more rain—I was texting Thunderbolt. He's out of the country doing freelance work and between our travel schedules I haven't seen him in weeks. Gonna admit that I miss him —a lot. I'm even ninety-nine percent resolved that I'm going to tell him how I really feel when get gets back.

Anyway, back to Mr. PT.

This, ladies, is probably the high quality guy so many are looking for—lack of punctuality notwithstanding.

Has not just a job, but a career. Check.

Loves his daughter and his family. Check.

Is open to a long term relationship and marriage. Check.

Is in good shape. Check.

Is working on improving his body, mind, and spirit. Check.

And yet, zero chemistry. I don't have a solid reason as to why. My first thought was maybe it's because he's not a creative. If we love in other people what we love in ourselves, then it's no wonder I'm attracted to storytellers.

A creative, a storyteller, he was not. He likes food, wine, travel. I mean right before he saw me, he was hanging with his grandfather for fucks sake. He'd even taken a break from serious dating while his daughter was going through the awkward years. Now that she's more interested in friends than her parents, he's interested in dating.

I want to say more. Offer an explanation as to why I, who am looking for a long term relationship with someone who's not crazy, could not gin up interest. Now all the experts will tell you that there's no reason not to go on a second date. Though punctuality, it turns out, may be my deal breaker. I'm thinking about it...as a possibility. I, at least, left the door open.

Me: Thanks so much for a lovely afternoon of great conversation. Have a wonderful evening. I'll be having soup...

(as an aside, we both have a ridiculous love of soup)

Mr. PT: I'm soooo jealous of you ☺ ... well thank you I enjoyed all of our conversations ... anytime you want company for anything I'm open to simple adventures ... keep in touch (rose emoji).

Simple adventures. I could invite him out for soup. We could talk. Hang out. Talk about kids or California or life. He appears to have the two most important qualities for a relationship, emotional intelligence and emotional availability. If I don't choose a second date, then maybe I don't have either of those. It's food for thought.

FORTY-SEVEN

Superstition

DECEMBER 13 (FRIDAY).

I INVITED Mr. PT for soup. Because I wanted to see up close and personal what exactly a normal, open guy looked like. So maybe I could study him like a specimen. Maybe use him as a roadmap to figure out exactly what I should be looking for.

My head tells me that I need a guy like Mr. PT. My heart, well, my heart is a liar. It tells me I need Thunderbolt.

How is he, you might ask? I know you didn't, but I'll tell you. He's fine. He's in the city where I was born. He had a great thing happen to him.

On Monday I was prying myself out of bed after reading too late and getting ready to go to the gym when my watch vibrated on my arm.

Thunderbolt: I literally just got the email that the film was accepted.

Obviously this is the middle of the conversation we were having about whether his film had been accepted into a major festival abroad. There may have been screaming and jumping up and down in my kitchen, then I did...nothing.

For the life of me I couldn't think what I should say. Yeah, I know, 'congratulations' would have worked. and I may have said that two or three hours later in between a Trader Joe's stop and a second supermarket on Santa Monica Boulevard. I thought long and hard over the last week about why in the hell it was so hard to respond to his text. Something that should have been easy was hard. I'm a grown ass woman who was flustered by a text.

Lots of meditation and driving—because Los Angeles—led me to the answer.

It's fear.

Fear of rejection.

Fear of humiliation.

Fear that this guy that I've finally admitted to myself that I like will wake up from whatever fog he's in and realize that I'm too much, crazy. Too much work. Too much fear bundled into a middle aged female body and decide that he's done.

The best way to fix a problem like that? Focus on something or someone else. Like this very normal guy, with a very normal job, who wants a very normal relationship. Someone who is the complete opposite of me.

Me: This spot: Beverly Soon Tofu is one of my go-to favorites. No frills, but amazing soup. If you're game maybe we could me up at 3? I have to be in Santa Monica at 7 or so on Friday night for a talk at the Unplug Meditation studio out there...
Mr. PT: Perfect see you there at 3 for our soup date.

Look at that. A reasonable and normal response. No random 'hi' no weird back and forth. Just straight up clear communication.

I was even thinking of trying it myself. I had a lot of time yesterday between lunch with a friend and an event at a public library branch to think about what I should do next. So I composed a text to Thunderbolt:

Me: Hey there. I've missed hanging out with you.
Really looking forward to seeing you when you're
back…

Haven't sent it. Been thinking about it for about a minute or a few hours. Twenty-six hours to be exact. Then…

Sent it while I was waiting for Mr. Pt.

No response.

I've refused to check the iMessage read receipt.

Then I went on to wait to start my second date with Mr. PT.

He was late.

Half hour.

Seriously?

When I put down my phone, one of the waitresses came over.

"Still waiting?"

"Traffic," I said.

"A date?"

I nodded.

"Let me move you to a better table," she said. Then she did.

I got a great table in a cozy corner of one of my favorite Korean tofu soup places. When he finally came in, he sat next to me and not across from me. I wish I could say why that felt too intimate. I read him the menu and then we ordered soup.

I love soup. I consumed the very warm and tasty soup. He talked. I talked. I thought about Thunderbolt. Like I had to pull my mind out of the clouds to try to focus on him. The only person that made me forget about anything else was Classic Car Guy. Even when Mr. PT complimented me.

Sat close enough to touch, I just couldn't muster up any feeling.

I asked a lot of questions. Got a lot of answers.

He's a physical therapist because he had a really bad accident when he was young and stupid and admired how various therapists put him back together.

He went to tantric speed dating because he doesn't do online dating apps. Obviously I'm all about the apps, but I didn't get into my year of sexual exploration. He's only interested in meeting people in a more organic meet up. I'm not sure a singles meet up meets the definition of organic. Again I kept my own counsel.

I want to travel to Iceland or Egypt in March. He spends weekends in Victorville. You'll have to google that location, because I'm not.

It's just not a match. I need someone who respects me with punctuality. I want someone who thinks more about art, music, museums, and the bigger issues in life. I love conversations about political theory, renaissance art, and foreign travel. So he's nice, but not for me.

He likes time with his family and eating and drinking and weekend casino trips. I can't even begin to see how something like that would work. It's a life completely different from my own.

Mr. PT hugged me. He kissed me on the mouth. Twice.

Then I got into my car and took myself home to finish chapter nine of the book I'm working on.

I sent a lovely thank you, then took myself to a class called Meditation for Better Sex. It was interesting. Sex with Thunderbolt is already amazing, so it was kind of an icing on the cake type of class. I'm not sure I'm ready to try the techniques from the class. I'd need the kind of intimacy that I don't have with anyone...yet.

My plan? To spend the rest of the weekend with myself. I

have to finish writing a book. Work on a marketing plan for 2020. Maybe choose a place to travel with my son for Spring break. Think about love and how to find it with someone who matches my...as we woo woo Californians would say...spiritual vibration.

I'm still one hundred percent hopeful.

FORTY-EIGHT

The Sad Holidays

DECEMBER 20.

I'VE NEVER BEEN a person who was sad during the holiday season. For now I'm that person. I don't know if it's the holidays, or time without my son, or the silence from Thunderbolt, but I've done nothing by cry for the last five days.

I cried when I woke up each morning, shutting myself in the kitchen so my nine year old son didn't hear my sobs. I cried after I dropped my son off at school. Blasting music in my car did nothing to drown out my thoughts or feelings. I cried when I tried to eat, or write. I cried in the shower.

I told my therapist that I wanted the sadness to end. For years I stuffed my feelings. I applied copious amounts of food. When I got fat, I applied copious amounts of exercise, and a super restrictive diet that took all of my time to manage leaving no time to feel my feelings. I applied alcohol, but feared that second drink having grown up with an alcoholic, so that never took hold. I applied shopping until my closet was full to bursting with clothes, shoes, and purses.

I've stopped doing it all. The divorce diet of no appetite has made me slim again. I can't get excited about buying purses, shoes, or clothes. They all seem superfluous, plus I still don't have space in my closet. I don't want alcohol. I can't think of anything that will make me feel better.

Supposedly this will pass, but it feels like I'm drowning in my own tears.

♥

TWO YEARS AGO, I bought five stacking rings in silver, rose, and yellow gold. Etched in them is the Maya Angelou quote, "When people show you who they are, believe them, the first time."

I got these rings, because the one mistake I continue to make over and over again is wanting to believe people are different than they tell me they are.

Why all this introspection? Because I've been all over the map about Thunderbolt, but our 'situationship' is ending just as I thought it would.

After I sent that text, I got radio silence. Please stop me if you know how this is going to turn out, because it took me a good week to figure it out. He texted when he landed:

Thunderbolt: Just back from nyc. Glad to be home.
Me: Glad to have you back in town.

I didn't say anything more. I was arranging a play date for my son. Baking with him and his friends, helping him with his second book report of the year. Watching his school's holiday concert. In other words, I was doing my mom thing. But I drop my kid off on Friday for the weekends, so I sent this text on Thursday.

Me: How's your Friday looking? Are you free tomorrow?

And you know what? My texts have been delivered. (Thank you iMessage delivery notification). He hasn't read a single one since he landed. (Thank you iMessage read receipts).

I know that silence means, at least to me. I remember it from six months ago with Classic Car guy.

I know that we're not supposed to tell ourselves stories about the actions other people take. What they do is only supposed to be information, that it's not about us, but about them. But I have to fill in those blanks, that silence, with something. He said he was waiting for the perfect woman who would cause a thunderbolt to course through him. That's the information I had. I thought I could be that person. That's a leap I probably shouldn't have taken.

He said in more than one way more than one time that he didn't want a relationship. I talked myself into a belief that I could have a relationship with someone who's emotionally unavailable. That was my conclusion.

Again.

Dear Universe: I got the message. I won't do this a third (or fourth, or maybe even sixth) time.

I will get it together in the next year, the next decade that will come in just eleven days.

On Oprah's Super Soul Conversations podcast this week, she featured Houston pastor Joel Osteen. He said, "What follows ***I am*** will always come looking for you."

This year, I've said about myself: I am unworthy. I am undeserving. I am a woman who accepts crumbs. I am an abuse victim. I am never going to get divorced because my ex won't let me go. I am too old for love. I am too much for a good man.

And all of those things have come to pass.

For 2020, I am a new person.

I am a great storyteller.

I am the best mother I can be.
I am a survivor.
I am worthy.
I am loved.

FORTY-NINE

Upon Reflection

DECEMBER 29.

ON THE THURSDAY BEFORE SUNDAY, I got a text from Thunderbolt. After a week of crying and feeling sorry for myself, I was chilling between therapy which makes me feel zen and looking up where to send a couple of my designer purses for repair.

I was sitting on my dining room banquette and had my feet up while I was filling time between my morning and the Boxing Day afternoon matinee of *Jitney*, a Tony award-winning August Wilson revival that was downtown at the Mark Taper Forum.

Thunderbolt: Hey sorry holidays got crazy.
Me: Hope you had a great Christmas.
Thunderbolt: Pretty mellow. You?
Me: On the whole pretty good. I don't have my kid for Xmas break so a lot of catch up work and writing.
Thunderbolt: Nice. Home today? How about an afternoon rendezvous?
Me: I'm running out of the door right now to see a

play. The Tony-winning revival of Jitney. If later then sure...
Thunderbolt: K I'll hit you up later.

Usually, I'd tell him when I'm home and he'd show up five minutes later. I didn't text because I was still on the fence about how I was going to approach my FWB with having feelings. I'd written him off and with one text he'd pulled me back in. I wanted to kiss him and kill him at the same time. That didn't feel like the right mindset.

On Sunday, though, I was ready.

Me: Busy later? Want to hang out?
Thunderbolt: Yeah let's hang. When's good?
Me: 8? Finished writing early today...
Thunderbolt: Cool yep.

"Would you like a beverage?" I asked after he made himself comfortable on one of the kitchen stools at the breakfast bar.

"Nah, I'm good."

Nearly every time Thunderbolt comes to my apartment, he does a little tour noting what's changed since was last there. First, he picked up my holiday card. It was the last one I planned to save for posterity along with some extra envelopes. It's a picture of me and my son taken by a professional photographer in Griffith Park in the fall.

"Who is this?"

"Seriously?" I looked from him to the card in his hand. "It's me and my son."

He held the card closer to greater scrutiny. "It doesn't look like you. Maybe because I don't see you smile often."

The card looks exactly like me. After thinking about it, I'm pretty sure I saw him that night not two or three hours after that picture was taken. I let that go because I already knew it was going to be a weird night.

Then he picked up the top of my butter dish. Let me tell you about this butter dish. It's red. It's Le Crueset. I bought it from Macy's when I moved to West Hollywood because I left the butter dish with my ex.

Every single time he comes over, he brings up two things: how neat my living space is and this damned butter dish.

"I can't believe this butter dish," he said.

"What is it about this dish?"

"It's Le Creuset."

"It's a butter dish."

"It's signaling."

"What am I signaling with a red ceramic butter dish."

"That it's expensive."

One issue that comes up between us time and again is income disparity. I earn more than he does. Probably significantly more. When a friend was talking about an article she'd read about Thunderbolt in the *Hollywood Reporter* or *Rolling Stone*, she mentioned that he'd gone broke making his movie and that the women who were dating him, dumped him.

I haven't read the article because if I take even a shallow dive into his public life, I'll go in and never come out. It's the same reason I avoided Googling Classic Car Guy until we broke up. I can become obsessive about researching people. I'd rather have them tell me about themselves.

When I first met Thunderbolt, he mentioned that he was embarrassed to be his age, now forty-three, and still living in a small rent-controlled studio. I now know he sold his car because he needed the money (my friend said it was in the news feature). He said that his biggest fear was becoming like his half brother in Baltimore who's both, in his words, not mine, fat and marginally employed.

I like nice things, and buy them for myself. I like to travel to foreign countries, and go to nice restaurants and the theater. I'm not going to say that these things intimidate him because I don't assume to understand anyone's feelings. I'll just say that he talks about my lifestyle often, the fundamental argument against which is best encapsulated by this butter dish.

This money discussion can sometimes go off the rails, and because I was nervous about the talk I wanted to have with him, I cut it short by suggesting we just go to bed. Which we did. What I've always liked about Thunderbolt is that he's a generous lover. Like seriously giving and good. Tonight wasn't his most generous. I didn't push it either because I was too busy being nervous about telling him about my feelings after the sex. I deliberately didn't tell him before because I knew after talking to him it may be the last time we had sex.

After the sex we lay in my bed and talked about movies he'd recommend for me. We talked about the book I'm writing now and some of the other books I've written. He often asks such specific questions that I wonder if he's putting together a dossier. My ex never asked a thing about me, so I'm not used to a man's interest in my life. Anyway, the conversation drifted until I ended up talking about this slow speed wreck of a conversation I witnessed. It's a story I sometimes tell because it's was one of the most fascinating peeks into other's people's lives I've ever witnessed.

About five years ago I was writing in a coffee shop after I'd dropped my son off at kindergarten. Sometimes I camped out for an hour to avoid traffic. If I left after dropoff, I'd be on the road for an hour. If I waited for an hour, the ride home would only be twenty minutes. Writing always trumps driving for me.

It was a tiny coffee shop with few tables, but close to his school. I pulled up, went in, and ordered myself a latte. Then I took my laptop to the back and set up to write.

Before I could get into my book a man took the seat next to me. I probably noticed him because he was nervous. Fidgeting.

Moving the table around. Moving his coffee around. Getting up and getting a large ice water after he'd already gotten coffee. It was in an area of Los Angeles where no one dresses up. So his button-down shirt and blazer were an anomaly.

Eventually, a woman joined him. She was attractive but super casual. Southern California is casual, but even in a jeans culture, there are layers of casual. There's the button down and blazer casual, like him. Then there are the sweats and t-shirt a woman might wear on a laundry day. It was this woman's laundry day, and a no-makeup day, and a put her hair up in a bun on the top of her head day.

The man gets her a coffee. Then he leans in. Let's call him Julio and her Elizabeth.

"Elizabeth, I think we could have a great future together. I just bought a house. My job is stable. I think it's time to settle down."

Elizabeth looked like she wished she'd already drunk the coffee in her hand, and maybe another, and a better night's sleep, and somewhere to run. She had that 'deer in the head-lights' look that made even me uncomfortable. She leaned away. As far as a straight-backed chair would let her lean.

"I'm still in college, Julio" she started. "I'm not sure where I'm going in life."

It went on like this for a good half hour. I got no writing done because I may have been live texting it for a group of writer friends. The best thing about writer friends. They're avoiding writing too and are almost always available for a good group text session.

For some reason, I was telling this story to Thunderbolt.

"So what was the guy like?" he asked.

"Earnest?" I shrugged. That is the single best description.

"No, like on a scale of one to ten? What was he?"

"I don't know maybe a five or six?" I said. "But maybe not

for her. Maybe he had some other qualities that made him super attractive to her."

"Didn't sound like it," Thunderbolt said while he stretched his naked leg in the air.

"Do you know the advice that single women receive. That I've received about five times in the last week?"

"What?"

"That we should consider dating men that we find less than attractive because attraction can grow."

"Are you serious? I think you have to start high because attraction only wanes in a relationship." That was an interesting take, to say the least. I had to wonder where that put me, but I didn't ask.

I turned to him, propped myself up on my elbow so I could see him better.

"So what are you?"

"Me?"

"On a scale of one to ten."

"If it's only looks? I'm a pretty good looking guy. So I'd say 8, but if other stuff is included..."

"Then?"

"Look, I'm good looking. I'm incredibly funny and really creative. I'm chill but driven. I'm really good at sex. With that whole package. I'm a solid nine out of ten."

Now, in my brain, I'd promised myself that I'd have that talk about feelings with him. What in the hell could I say to that? But I'd promised myself, so I looked him in the eye.

"I might agree with that assessment. Before you go, I have to talk to you. I promised myself I'd do this. So..."

So we got dressed. Him in clothes, me in pajamas. We walked back into the kitchen.

"What do you want to say?"

"Here's the thing," I stuttered to a stop. Regrouped. "I

think I caught feelings for you. I know this fucks up this thing we have going, but I had to say it."

"I think that's the difference between men and women," he said.

"That's not true," I said. "I was fine for months until it wasn't."

"This casual thing," he gestured around my apartment where ninety-nine percent of our situationship had taken place, "is all that's going to happen."

"Right, okay," I said. I knew those words were coming. He'd said as much many times. I had to discount his behavior and only listen to what he said.

"I hope you're still dating. That this hasn't stopped you from finding someone," he added.

"I've been dating the whole time, you know that." He'd asked me about it enough times.

"And I didn't mind that. I told you that."

There was nothing more to say. I wanted to go outside and have sushi with him. Spend more time with him. He didn't want that. Impasse is the word for that one.

"Well, do you want some fruit before you go," I asked because he was eyeing the bowl of berries on my counter.

"Sure." He popped one or two into his mouth. "This is good. Different. What is it?"

"I don't know. It was on display at the store. Threw away the package."

"I think you need to reflect," he said looking me in the eye.

"On what?"

"If you want to continue to do this casual thing."

"It's fine. We can... You're not leaving town for a few weeks. I thought maybe—"

He interrupted me.

"If after reflection you want to do this again, just hit me up. I'm always in the neighborhood."

I decided that there was nothing else to say, so I stood and started walking toward the mud-room. He followed.

"Have a happy new year," I said. "Enjoy your family-friendly party." He'd mentioned being invited to a party with kids. He figured he'd be back home before midnight.

I opened the back door for him, since he'd driven, then he pulled me in for a kiss on the way out. Not a good-bye kiss like most time, but a kiss like he was going to stay. Like he was going to see me again.

I wasn't thrilled with his parting words, but I am reflecting. According to everything I'm reading, I need to clean him out of my life in order to bring someone new in. It was lesson 8, the lesson of the day from Calling in "The One": 7 Weeks to Attract the Love of Your Life. I needed to heed the author's words.

I called on all my friends because it was hard. Hard because letting him go is probably the right thing for my sanity. Hard because I want nothing more than to call him to come over and have more wine and more chat and more of the good kind of sex we'd perfected. Hard because I was alternating between meditation and spinning and yoga and crying. I put before you, their words of wisdom.

Pierce (my painter friend from the art show and ill fated date with The Hiker): I say-Good for you. I know that must have been very, very hard-not intellectually, but emotionally. Physically. Stay strong. You don't need to bring people into 2020 that are unable to love you the way you need to be loved.

Trust.

Honor.

Respect.

Partnership.

Equality.

Love.

· · ·

THE MOVIE PRODUCER: I'm guessing you know this (and it doesn't take away the hurt), but his inability to have an adult relationship has nothing to do with you, or your value and everything to do with him.

The Bestseller: I'm sorry. I know that's not what you were hoping for. I can't help but believe there's a new guy out there. One you haven't met yet, who's ready for what you want. I think you can have sex and chat with Thunderbolt without stunting your growth. As long as you don't let it stop you from seeing other people. It's only bad if it's taking up space that should be filled by what you really want. But that seems like a down the road decision. Sex and chatting with the FWB while you date other lovely men seems very reasonable. And when one of those lovely men takes your attention away from the FWB guy, you can fondly kiss him good bye. Expect him to want a serious thing with you then, though. It's him, not you. You don't have to figure him out. Just recognize his behavior and don't let it throw you. It's okay for us to do things that just feel good and trust that the grown ass men can look out for themselves.

The Traveler (from Taiwan): You're not trash, so don't let anyone treat you like that. You are fucking amazing, smart, interesting, and have so much to give. Please know that. Thunderbolt might be great, but he obviously can't recognize or respect all that you have to offer. I'm so glad you're having that hard talk with him. Bravo. I love you, friend. You're not alone.

FIFTY

The One Man Show

JANUARY 10.

ONE OF THE men I'd matched with at tantric dating, I'd also matched with on Tinder. At the beginning of this week, I slowly but surely turned my dating profiles back on. I think I'd turned them off in November before I traveled to Houston for one week and Hawaii for another. I was finding them frustrating. The same issues that had been there all along somehow seemed magnified in the fall. Men don't want to meet in person.

I can't stress enough how much I don't want to text or chat with someone I don't know. It's enough to keep up with the people I know and love dearly. I have no desire to add unknown people who may be married, who I may never meet in person, who may be skeevy to that mix.

All this to say that I was going through my old matches for the last few months, deleting those I decided weren't going to get a second look when I came across The Flautist.

He'd been one of the twenty men I'd met when speed dating. He was good looking in a swarthy way. Not my thing, looks-wise, but I'm always trying to not be as narrowly focused on my very particular type.

I wasn't a fan of the fact that he came to the speed dating event wearing a fedora, but I thought our two to five-minute conversation was interesting. He has a boutique purse design business. He plays the flute and saxophone and he is a semi-professional photographer. I love creative people so I sent him an email post speed date and we had a bit of back and forth.

I'd not made an effort to keep that up when his first ask was could I apply my writing skills to help him with his boutique's website. While I love my job as a writer, I don't really have a desire to help someone I don't know well with theirs. But when I saw him on Tinder and looked at his photos—he has professional ones taken often—I gave him another shot.

> **Me:** OMG. I just realized who you are... Tantric speed dating anyone...
> **The Flautist:** Hey! I was just thinking about you this must be a sign LOL.

We chatted on the Tinder app. A star of an HBO show was going to accessorize with one of his purses on the Golden Globes' red carpet.

When I'd messaged him, he'd just delivered it to her and was feeling pretty good. The app conversation went well enough that I decided to ask him to go to the one-man show I'd bought tickets for that morning.

Before Friday, he texted me some pictures from the red carpet with the actress sporting his bag. I was hopeful after that text. Hopeful that it would be a good date with an interesting creative person who was actively pursuing his art.

I put on a dress, bought new knee-high suede boots, and made the drive to the Santa Monica Playhouse. The one-man show was put on by a comedian named Josh Sundquist based on his book, *We Should Hang Out Sometime*. Before the show,

Sundquist had sent an email asking attendees to send him an Instagram message with three emojis that best described our love lives. I immediately picked up my phone and sent him an eggplant, a broken heart, and a facepalm.

Because I'm eternally prompt, I got to the show exactly on time. The Flautist came and gave me a quick hug and sat next to me. I wanted to be more excited, but I kind of wasn't. He smelled like smoke and had too many accessories. A hat, a scarf, a bag. It was all a lot for me—admittedly a person who may be given to over-accessorizing.

Fortunately, the theater opened and we took our seats in the second row. Half of the last few shows I've attended have had some kind of video projection of some kind. This was no exception. When I finally paid attention to what was on screen, I realized it was my Instagram direct message.

Josh: So an eggplant broke your heart. Vegetables can be so dangerous. Are you at the show yet?
Me: I'm right here...
Josh: Oh, right here? No way.
Me: Yes way.
Josh: Who are you here with?
Me: Guy in a hat.
Josh: Please send a selfie.

I took a selfie with the Flautist and messaged it. It appeared on the stage wall.

Josh: I see you... You look good in blue. Who is the guy in the hat. Is he your lover?
Me: No...this is awkward. First date.
Josh: First date. No way.
Me: Yes way.

Josh: Don't worry this convo is just between you and me. 100% privacy. How is the date so far? I like his hat.
Me: It's been 10 minutes.
Josh: Is he on Instagram, tell him to message me.
Me: He's doing it now.
Josh: Great. I'll let you know what he says about you...

Personally, I found this pre-show display hilarious. The Flautist, not so much. He was not game to go along with the humor. When Josh came out in person and asked how we met, The Flautist remained quiet. I finally fessed up to tantric Speed dating which earned a hearty laugh from the audience. I enjoyed the rest of the show. The Flautist made snarky remarks under his breath.

After the show, he wanted to get some tea, so we walked over to the Third Street Promenade and went to a Coffee Bean and Tea Leaf. He was frustrated with the selection of teas and the selection of sweeteners. I probably should have called it a night then, but as always I dragged things on too long.

I reluctantly chose some chamomile and sat across from him in the harsh fluorescent light.

Last year I regularly watched Jada Pinkett Smith's Red Table Talk. During an episode where she featured comedian Tiffany Haddish, Haddish talked about her 'dick pic book.' Her conclusion after observing lots of penises was this, check a man's hands. If his hands aren't groomed, his cock probably wasn't either.

Long story short, the Flautist did not have clean hands or fingernails. I think that was all the information I needed. Grooming was not his top priority, though it's of critical importance to me.

I could write more paragraphs about the fact that he'd had few relationships because the women he dated always found him wanting. How he was depressed about spending so much time alone or that he'd put three hundred thousand miles on his fifteen-year-old Prius. None of that mattered. I didn't need a moment more to know that we weren't a match.

I was hoping to go on a date Saturday night with another cute guy I'd matched with on Tinder. His criteria before meeting in person was that we have a phone conversation. He'd called me several nights in a row, but I didn't answer the phone. I explained to him that I had a child and dinner and homework and helping a nine-year old bathe. 'Could I talk after that?' he asked.

No, I told him. I didn't get into the fact that I fell straight to sleep after all that because my son can be exhausting.

He called during the one-man show. Fortunately, I had the phone on vibrate. He texted on Saturday morning on the way to spinning class.

Him: Can I call you? What kind of show was it? (selfie included) Wyd. Talk or text?
Me: One man show. He's a stand up who did kind of an autopsy about his dating life. I'm at SoulCycle waiting for my spinning class to start in a few minutes.
Him: Talk? Or text?

At this point my annoyance level was high. I'd read a quote in a Jodi Rempel article right before driving to the gym. She said, 'We can choose when to say yes and how to say no.' I decided boundaries were in order.

Me: Class starts in a few. Then I have some errands to run and work to get through today. I'd love to meet up for drinks later today. If you're uncomfortable with that without a phone conversation I understand. But then I think we're not a match. I prefer to talk in person. Let me know if you're game to meet. If not no harm no foul.

Him: I prefer in person too. Just like to have one conversation before meeting. No rush.

I didn't have to read between the lines. We were never going to meet. I'm not saying that his need to have a phone conversation before driving two or three miles wasn't reasonable. It just wasn't going to happen because it was unreasonable for me.

In a year of dating, I've gleaned zero from awkward phone conversations. That's not how I was going to spend my time. I'd rather write a book.

FIFTY-ONE

The Foreigner

JANUARY 31.

IN TWO HOURS, I'm going out on my first date in two weeks. Except for a second one night stand with the Actor a few days after the new year, it's been quiet.

An unexpected dating hiatus.

I think I've spent the time seeing plays, working on a side project, and trying not to think about Thunderbolt. At the last, I succeed about sixty-two percent of the time.

I have one of those five year diaries. I can't remember which guru recommended it, but writing a few lines every day of the year and being able to look back at your life over five years felt like a good idea when I purchased the book in January 2018.

The unfortunate consequence is that I came across diary entries from last year that talked about when I first met Thunderbolt. I'd forgotten I'd written about him or had become that infatuated with him at such an early stage until I saw them over the last few days when I journaled in the morning. My brain had forged a connection that I'd thought was subconscious. Obviously, I'd been into him from the beginning no matter how many times I'd tried to talk myself out of it.

Last weekend was also the big movie festival.

Thunderbolt is a big one to post Instagram stories, but not actual posts that would linger. It's kind of a reflection of how I see him. All intense in the moment until it disappears and I'm left wondering if what I experienced was really true.

I woke up Saturday morning to Insta Stories of him alone drinking coffee and of the cold often barren looking scenery. For some reason, that aloneness made me sad.

I wish I could pinpoint why a solitary cappuccino pulled me back in, but it did. For the sake of my anxiety or sanity or both, I had to unfollow him on that platform. I'd already muted him on Facebook. Unfollowing came too late because he was already in my thoughts. Couple that with my ex having one of his crazy messaging weeks and I quickly spiraled down into the land of disquiet and Xanax.

Against the backdrop of all that, I've been meeting men on the apps. The cute long-haired ones? They want to text too much. I want to meet in person. That fact communicated with them somehow makes them disappear. Sound kind of familiar? I'd like to think I was learning my lessons earlier this time.

Enter, the Foreigner.

As you know, I spend my summer in a small faraway country. I was swiping through OkCupid, when I saw one of the introductions you can get from someone who 'likes' you even when you don't like them back yet.

The Foreigner: Hi Jolie, so fascinated reading your profile. I am from [the small country], so the pics from there made my heart skip a beat! Would love to know how/why you spent so much time there! I have never been to the places you want to go to, but I would happily weigh in just so that I can pique your interest. Except I am kinda authentic, real and don't like to cheat. No matter how much I would looove to connect with you. I grew up on/in theater - you probably know that the [small country] has the highest number of theaters per capita in the world. If you didn't, talk to me! It is also possible that you may have seen my uncle's musical there - if you saw any local performances. I don't know what else to say - please read my profile and I will hopefully hear from you! [prayer hands emoji]

I love my time abroad. I'm usually there with my son three or four times a year, so I have to say I was intrigued. I only glanced at his picture before I responded. One of my new year dating schemes was to meet someone from that country.

My theory was that I would have to spend far less time explaining my love for that place if I met someone who was already from there or who spent time there like I did. But it is a small country which means that there aren't a lot of people from there out in the world.

Their last mass migration was in the nineteen fifties. Fortunately there's a little consulate here in Los Angeles and a little social/cultural organization. I've been meaning to join it, but my son and writing have kept me busy.

I responded about twelve hours after he sent that message —which for me is close to nearly immediately. I told him how much I loved the country, how I'd come to spend so much time there, and what theater I enjoyed there. Of course, it turns out that he grew up about a half-mile from my place there. We chatted, online, about theater and poetry and all the things I like.

When it comes to being online, we got on quite well. So with that, I agreed to a date tonight, only four days after we connected. Unlike everyone else, he was not one to let grass grow under his feet. He's not close, about twenty-five miles away from West Hollywood (which may as well be a thousand in Southern California). But he offered to come to me.

Like the Sociologist, he was chivalrous, so I accepted that offer. I no longer give two figs about whether or not I somehow offend Thunderbolt's sensitive nature by dating under his nose. With that decision behind me, we're meeting at Tart. I haven't been there since my night with Drummer Boy.

This one...this one will not end like that one. I promise you that.

I have not reconciled dates with nice guys and sex with not nice guys. I'd love to find sexy, cute and nice in one package, but I haven't yet.

Not so ironically, The Sociologist (who shares the same first name as the Foreigner—small country, smaller name pool) texted me this week, asking about my return.

> **The Sociologist:** heyy, how are you? when are you coming?
> **Me: I** was thinking about you. I'll be there in March. Bought tickets last week...
> **The Sociologist:** we should meet then, i'm missing you ❤
> **Me:** Absolutely.
> **The Sociologist:** :)) 😶

This was, I think, a lovely exchange. It reminded me of all the reasons I'd loved having him as my summer friends with benefits.

Instead of basking in the glow of that exchange, I compared it to Thunderbolt. I said I missed spending time with him and that spiraled out into a slow speed break up. Why??—I thought as I cried in my car while driving down a

Los Angeles boulevard toward a work meeting—couldn't he have been that cool? Why couldn't it have been easier with him?

I tried not to dwell, but there it was. All the feelings again. How much I liked him. How much I liked spending all those evenings together. How much I enjoyed talking about my books and his movie.

This is the frame of mind I'm in. My date is in less than ninety minutes. I'm going to get up and away from this keyboard, primp or prep for my date with a guy who seems nice and available, and try not to think about the guy whose halfway in asshole mode often and who was up until now, the best sex I'd ever had.

♥

IT'S after midnight as I write this. Our dinner reservation was for seven-thirty.

The Foreigner was on time. He drove any number of miles from Long Beach and he was...not one minute late. In many ways, it was the best first date I've had in a long time. We had a lot in common. He likes plays and museums. He has a photography hobby that he started at about the same time I started mine. He didn't think I talked too much. Although, let me tell you. I talk too much. If you listened to that podcast I did, you heard that.

It's so funny, how I feel right now. I want to do what I usually do in this space.

Download.

Give you the dirty deets.

Talk to you as if you're one of my girlfriends.

And for once.

For once.

I kind of want to keep it to myself.

Savor it.
Moon over what could be.
Because this feels like...
It could be something.
Real.

About the Author

JOLIE MOORE
Crazy Beautiful Love

I write crazy, beautiful love stories because I believe storytelling is magic. I love complicated heroines with secrets, strong heroes who fall hard, and a long winding road to happily ever after. When I'm not writing, I love to travel to witness the diverse tapestry of humanity, photograph the beauty of the world, visit museums, and watch live theater. I live in West Hollywood, California ten miles from the nearest airport.

I'm the host of *Fifty First Dates* the Podcast. I haven't found my own happily ever after, but I'm not done looking. Join me as I try to find my Mr. Right or maybe Mr. Right Now in Southern California.